THE OLD ORIGIN CHANGETH!

THE ENHANCEMENT AND EMBROIDERING OF SUPERHERO ORIGINS

EDITED BY

JIM BEARD

*For the Little Woman, the prime player in the never-changing origin
of my love.*

Jim Beard, Editor

Table of Contents

Change is the One Constant

A FOREWORD

By Dan DiDio

The origin of a superhero is a delicate thing. It explains why someone would choose to be a hero and how they got their powers to fight crime. Properly developed, it also helps to define the motivation behind a character's behavior. The more exciting and relatable the origin, the greater the chance for longevity and success.

Relatability comes in many forms. Personal tragedy, world situations, and age of the character, to mention a few. But as times change, relatability to established characters might change too. That's when creative choices need to be made, some choices that might not sit well with long-time fans.

Now personally, I love a good origin story. It's that moment of inception where you decide whether or not to bond to a character for life. When that bonding occurs, it's like we understand each other. I know what to expect from the characters, and the publisher knows I'm ready to follow their story from book to book and series to series. And while the quality may waver, and little details might change, the origin always remains as a character's north star, leading us all on the path chosen from the beginning.

So, I completely understand the frustration and betrayal felt when something I know better than my family's birthdays is revised and re-invented.

Unfortunately, as a former comics executive, I also know the necessity of updating origins in an attempt to keep up with changing times with the hope of attracting a newer audience. However, because time-stamped origins tend to date the hero, it can question their relevance if the origin feels set in antiquated ideals. Still, common sense usually dictates, "If it ain't broke, don't fix it." But "broke" is always up for interpretation, and "fix it" is a seductive drug for any creator or company looking to put a new stamp on an old character.

Now, some origins start broken. For example, DC Comic's the Creeper always generated a lot of goodwill and interest, primarily because of its creator. Still, his origin was so straight-out bonkers that any creator following the original run usually ignores or tries to reinvent it. Yet regardless of how silly the Creeper's origin was—a news reporter in a yellow and green Halloween costume with a lion's mane is shot and is given healing powers by injection after a button that can transform his clothes into his costume is implanted in his stomach—every time someone tried to change it, the change never stuck. Mainly because it never mattered much in the first place. But for the origins that do matter, they become iconic.

Superman rocketed to Earth as a baby and is probably better known by most people than the name of the company that publishes his comic. Not only does this origin define him, but it has also become a template for similar characters from other companies when they want their character to evoke the same feel as Superman. And even though he was created more than eighty years ago, Superman seems more relevant today than at the time of his creation. It makes you wonder why anyone would even attempt to change it. Yet, every few years or so, someone does, and like with any origin's retelling, the reason tends to vary.

We can blame progress. As science advances, the conceptual science of a character's origin might seem antiquated or downright silly. So, a scientific upgrade might be needed.

We can blame the calendar. Fans can suspend belief overpowers and abilities, but a thirty-year-old character born eighty years ago, is, oddly, hard to accept. Especially if that character were involved in historical events and moments, they would refer to constantly. This is, of course, for the characters that are supposed to age normally, (like Nick Fury) and not one that is purposely out of time (Capt. America). Still, as time passes, origins need to change, Vietnam becomes Afghanistan, and most stories built on World War II are slowly written out of the books. (Although…you can be sure we still keep seeing Superman throw a 1937 DeSoto, even if flying cars become a reality.)

We can always blame sales. Whenever sales lag on a title, there is always an attempt to turn the book around before cancellation. "Everything you know is false!" is a dramatic and overused catchphrase designed to reignite interest in a series people had lost interest in. It has a panicked goal of re-inventing the wheel with the hope of fixing, accidentally or not, whatever was broken. More often than not, the book winds up canceled even with the dramatic changes. Then after some time, the character can make its triumphant return, with its original origin back intact, or the origin changed even further, hoping to recapture past sales success.

Lastly, and most importantly, we must blame hubris. Everyone knows how to make it better. As creators, we are all guilty. In comics, there is no greater goal than to leave an imprint on a character who left his mark on you. A creator could use the other three excuses to change something firmly established, but the truth is, they wish to leave a mark, so they can be remembered along with the character they love. It's the goal of every writer and artist but only accomplished by the true greats.

It always comes down to understanding how and why an origin defined the hero and what connected the fans to the character. With Superman, it's not just the story of an alien on Earth but the story of the immigrant arriving in a new world. A world he will learn to call home. So, while the size and shape of his rocket might change to keep up with the times, the heart of his story can never change without disturbing the connection he has to the readers.

Fans are always worried about their characters being broken. But the truth is, they are nearly impossible to break. Change is the one constant in comics, whether making a character different or returning to its roots. Change and the illusion of change are essential tools of ongoing comic book storytelling, and if it doesn't work, that's okay. You can always go back to the beginning and start again.

For nearly twenty years, **Dan DiDio** served DC Comics in several roles, during which, his innovation and energy made him synonymous with the characters and publishing line.

Dan DiDio joined DC in January 2002 as Vice President, Editorial and quickly ascended into the role of Senior Vice President/ Executive Editor, DC Comics one year later. In that position, he directed the creative development and helped contemporize the superhero line of titles, to bring increased relevancy and diversity to the line. He was also responsible for attracting some of comics' top talent to DC and locking them into exclusive contracts to ensure quality books for the years to come.

DiDio was also an accomplished writer at DC Comics, having created and re-developed several comic series at DC, including *Sideways*, *OMAC*, *Phantom Stranger*, and *Metal Men*.

His efforts lead to a multi-year resurgence in sales with a string of best-selling, critically acclaimed titles including *Identity Crisis*, *Infinite Crisis*, the weekly series *52*, and *All-Star Superman*, and the revitalization of key franchises like *Batman*, *Wonder Woman*, and *Green Lantern*. In 2010 Dan DiDio was named Publisher of DC Entertainment, alongside Jim Lee. As Publisher, he directed and oversaw DC Entertainment's entire publishing business under its key three imprints, DC, Vertigo, and MAD.

Throughout his tenure, DiDio continued to work closely with DCE editorial and creative teams to develop compelling storylines and characters and spearheaded many of the comic industry's most successful publishing events, including the widely acclaimed relaunch of DC Comics with The New 52. He was instrumental in the creation of new imprints, like Gerard Way's Young Animal and Joe Hill's Hill House Comics and also worked with DCE's Creative Affairs and Warner Bros Film, Television and Animation teams to help coordinate the creative content of the comics with the media business.

When It's Time to Change, You've Got to Rearrange

AN INTRODUCTION

By Jim Beard

Change is hard.

That's especially true for comic book fans, I think. We like what we like, and when it changes, even a little bit, we're not happy. And we let people know it. That's a generalization, of course, but I feel okay making it because I'm a comic book fan and I'm not too fond of change. At my age, I know what I like, you see.

And here's the thing, we don't really have any business feeling like that, us comic book fans, because we're not really supposed to be here. What I mean by that is we were supposed to have our time reading the books and then move on. Comics were not originally created and designed for a lifetime hobby, for a decades-long love affair. They were meant to be childhood pleasures, not something we carry with us through the rest of our lives and keep acquiring and reading. Why? Because they have to change with the times, something we just don't want to see happen.

In a way, this book is a tribute to comic book companies. I actually feel real sympathy for the ones that have been around since the very beginning, the ones that have had to adapt or decay and eventually die. I have sympathy for them because they are the caretakers of legendary characters known around the world, characters that come with built-in expectations to always be recognizable—and yet they need to change, too. I can't quite imagine what it would be like to own a Superman or a Captain America, say, a property with such strong times to a place in time, a mood, a feeling, but "living" in a world that keeps jumping ahead and changing its moods and feelings. Adapt or decay and eventually die. That's what its all about. Keep up that balance between the core character and those crazy comic book fan expectations, not to mention the rest of the world's populace, too.

Change is hard.

The origins of this book do *not* involve change, by the way.

Back around 2010, after I had worked with a publisher on a book that was kind of about comics but more about television, I spent a little time dreaming up more concepts for more books, ones that were solely about comics. The idea for *this* book sprang up wholly formed: a look at the ever-changing origins of comic book superheroes. I thought it sounded pretty cool, and very unique. I still do.

Then, nothing. For whatever reasons I didn't pitch the project to that publisher or any other but tucked it away for future use. It stayed there in my back pocket for all these years until I formed my own publishing house, Becky Books, and wanted to do a book solely about comics. And let me tell you, in all this time the concept didn't change one single bit. This is exactly the way I dreamed it up. No change.

Here's what you're getting in *The Old Origin Changeth!*

Each essay in here is by a different writer, and in the words of Superman from *Justice League Unlimited*, they "all bring something different to the table." That's what I love about collaborations: I get a unique voice and approach from each one of them. The writers all had some guidelines, sure, but they were all told to come at their subjects in whichever way they choose. To me, that makes for a more personable essay.

So, you're going to get some opinions in these examinations of the biggest superhero concepts ever. You're going to get six different takes on how to talk about the changing origins of not only DC Comics' top-three titans, but also Marvel's sensational stars. I had a blast editing the book and bringing it all together. I like how things change in tone and feeling from essay to essay.

I hope you like change. You do, don't you?

Jim Beard became a published writer when he sold a story to DC Comics in 2002. Since that time, he's written official Star Wars and Ghostbusters comic book stories and contributed articles and essays to several volumes of comic book history. His prose work includes the novellas *Green Hornet: How Sweet the Sting*, and *Kolchak: The Last Temptation*; co-editing and contributing to *Planet of the Apes: Tales From the Forbidden Zone*; a story for *X-Files: Secret Agendas*; three books of essays on the 1966 Batman TV series; the Sgt. Janus occult detective series of novels; *Monster Earth*, a shared-world giant monster anthology series; and *Captain Action: Riddle of the Glowing Men*, the first pulp prose novel based on the classic 1960s action figure. Jim also provided regular content for Marvel.com, the official Marvel Comics website, for over seventeen years, and is now publisher at Becky Books and co-publisher at Flinch Books with John C. Bruening. Look for Jim on Amazon at www.amazon.com/author/jimbeard, on Facebook at www.facebook.com/thebeardjimbeard, and on Twitter at @writerjimbeard.

SUPERMAN

First Appearance: *Action Comics* #1, April 18th 1938

Superman and the Legion of Super-Origins

By Joseph Dilworth Jr.

The Past

The Man of Steel. The Metropolis Marvel. The Last Son of Krypton. An immigrant from another planet, sent to Earth by his parents, Jor-El and Lara, moments before Krypton's destruction. Imbued by Earth's yellow sun with powers and abilities far beyond those of mortal men. Guided by his adopted parents, Jonathan, and Martha Kent, he has used his godlike powers to help the helpless and defend the weak.

Starting as the young Superboy in Smallville, Clark Kent eventually became a reporter in Metropolis. Able to fly like a bird or a plane, and strong enough to literally move mountains and even planets. With Kryptonite his only weakness, he continues to fight for truth, justice, and the American way, as the costumed superhero, Superman!

Everyone knows the origin of the first super-powered crime fighter, right? But would it surprise you to know that most of the details weren't part of his original origin or that many of them have changed or even disappeared over the years? To top it all off, some of what is taken as given about the Man of Tomorrow didn't necessarily originate in the comics, having been first mentioned in other media and later incorporated into his ongoing story.

9

For a character who has existed for more than eight decades (and counting), there has been a lot that has been modified, discarded, and assumed about him and yet, at its very core, the origin of Superman has remained broadly consistent, at least in the pages of DC Comics' *Superman* and *Action Comics*. There could be a whole book written about how varied his past has been depicted across various novels, radio shows, theatrical films, movies serials, television series, lunch boxes, record albums, t-shirts, and volumes of marketing materials. For our purposes, though, we'll keep this examination focused on the imaginary tales of DC Comics.

The Golden Age: How It Started

"As a distant planet was destroyed by old age, a scientist placed his infant son within a hastily devised space-ship, launching it toward Earth! When the vehicle landed on Earth, a passing motorist, discovering the sleeping babe within, turned the child over to an orphanage. Attendants, unaware the child's physical structure was millions of years advanced of their own, were astounded at his feats of strength."

This is how Jerome "Jerry" Siegel and Joe Shuster introduced Superman to the world in the first issue of *Action Comics* in April 1938. Kicking off not only the continual adventures of the not-yet-nicknamed Man of Steel, but also the Golden Age of Comic Books, it is a rather humble beginning. It starts off as we all know: Launched from a distant planet as an infant, headed to Earth, landing on Earth and discovered by a passing motorist...so far, so good! Turned over to an orphanage...wait a second, where are Ma and Pa Kent? And having a physical structure millions of years advance? A little different, but workable.

"When maturity was reached, he discovered he could easily: Leap 1/8th of a mile; hurdle a twenty-story building...raise tremendous weights...run faster than an express train...and that nothing less than a bursting shell could penetrate his skin! Early, Clark decided he must turn his titanic strength into channels that would benefit mankind. And so was created…Superman! Champion of the oppressed, the physical marvel who had sworn to devote his existence to helping those in need!"

That skillset sounds remarkably more subdued than the Superman we all know today. Leaping buildings, picking up some heavy things and running faster than a train does not sound like the all-powerful, nigh-indestructible demi-god we read about every month. There is even a quick scientific explanation for "Clark Kent's Amazing Strength," pointing to the fact that ants can support hundreds of times their weight and that grasshoppers easily leap the equivalent of several city blocks. All of this is to reiterate how the people of Superman's planet could also exhibit similar traits when they reach maturity. Somehow.

The last part is certainly right, sworn to help those in need, but those powers could be had by any old superhero, right? Except at that time, there were no other superhuman characters in comics like him. Superman was the first and, for a few months at least, the only fantastically powered costumed crimefighter. This is where it all began. Every superhero comic book character can trace their lineage back to the Spring of 1938 and the introduction of Superman.

At the time, this first page of *Action Comics*, with its kinetic, colorful images and astounding displays of incredible abilities must have been very captivating. I mean, the proof of that is this very discussion over eight decades later! You may also be wondering how we got from that relative bombastic, yet rather low-key, start to the godlike being we all know today. The short answer is a lot of different writers as well as adaptations across different mediums. Much of that was driven by the comic books and therein lies the longer explanation. Superman's origin would be expanded and altered many times throughout the years. That would begin almost exactly one year later.

Seeking to capitalize on the overwhelming success and rapidly growing popularity of the character, National Allied Publications (as DC Comics was then known) published the first issue of a solo comic, *Superman*. *Action Comics* was an anthology title featuring several characters each month, but National understandably wanted to shine the spotlight on its star attraction. Intended to be a one-shot collection, but overwhelmingly popular enough to continue as an ongoing title, issue one of *Superman* featured reprinted Superman stories from the first year of *Action Comics*. However, it did contain new material from Siegel and Shuster in the form of an expanded origin story.

Now running two pages, some details were added regarding our hero's past. Right off the bat, Supes' home planet is identified by the name Krypton. This would be further expanded upon a few months later. A Superman newspaper comic strip launched in January 1939 (told you the guy was getting popular!), also by Siegel and Shuster, would name his biological parents as Jor-L and Lara-L and even reveal the name of Kal-L for the future Clark Kent. Those names would further change once introduced in Superman's comic book stories, but more on that later.

The "passing motorist" who discovered a baby in a spaceship now became the elderly Kents, with the missus getting a name-check as Mary. Much like Clark's Kryptonian parents, the Kent's name would go through some refining over the years. The ship that carried the infant to Earth self-destructs once the child is removed, conveniently removing the need to hide the other-worldly vehicle. Additionally, while the orphanage employees he is left with begins to realize they can't handle a super-powered tyke, the Kents return, wishing to adopt him. We learn that "the love and guidance of his kindly foster-parents was to become an important factor in the shaping of the boy's future." The Kents extoll upon a young Clark the idea he must hide his gifts, lest others become afraid of him, but to use his abilities to assist humanity when the time comes.

The description of his powers remains the same, still chalked up to the advanced extraterrestrial society he hails from, although he can now lift a car instead of a steel girder. We also learn that the Kents pass away before his debut as the champion of the oppressed, their deaths being a final determining factor in his resolve to help mankind.

It would be another ten years until the comic books retold Superman's origin. In fact, it would be the "10th Anniversary Issue!" of the *Superman* title, issue #53 that would give us the most detailed accounting of the Last Son of Krypton to date. On the first page, the readers are promised answers to the questions millions have been asking, namely, "Who is Superman? Where did he come from? How did he obtain his miraculous powers?" Writer Bill Finger and artists Wayne Boring and Stan Kaye revealed those answers in a ten-page feature.

After a summary of Superman's astounding abilities, which now include x-ray vision, flight, and the strength to lift a building, we flash back to the planet Krypton and its inhabitants. Here, Kryptonians are described as humans of high intelligence and magnificent physical perfection. Apparently, they are subjected to a greater force of gravity, with one of their scientists noting that on Earth, with its weaker gravity, a Kryptonian can take a step and leap over the tallest building or perhaps defy gravity entirely. This is a slight modification to Kryptonians already possessing abilities greater than Earthlings; at home, they are just like us.

We get introduced to Superman's parents, who are named Jor-El and Lara, a slight variation to their non-comic book debut mentioned earlier. These versions of their names were first used a few years earlier in a Superman prose novel, *The Adventures of Superman*. That same novel also revealed the elderly Kents as Eben and Sarah Kent, who are clearly named John and Mary in *Superman* #53. Additionally, a film serial that had premiered earlier in the year named the Kents as Eben and Martha. Confused yet? Well, it gets slightly worse.

A few years prior to this, wishing to further take advantage of the public's rabid demand for more Superman stories, National Periodicals debuted the adventures of Superboy in *More Fun Comics* #101 in 1945. In 1946, Superboy became the main feature in *Adventure Comics*, where he would remain for the next two hundred-plus issues. These stories would show us Clark Kent assuming his Superguise while in high school and using his powers and costumed identity to aid the community of Smallville, his Earthly hometown.

However, there is no mention of Clark being Superboy in the origin featured in the 1948-published *Superman* #53. There are scenes that show him developing some of his powers in his youth, but the story clearly shows him not becoming the costumed Superman until after he is an adult and John and Mary have died. There is wiggle room in that there is no explicit mention of him not being Superboy, but it seems like something that ought to be spelled out in an origin story, or at least mentioned.

The origin of Superman gets one more retelling and expansion in the Golden Age of Comic Books in the pages of *Action Comics* #158, published in 1951. This retelling worked Kryptonite into the mix, the deadly mineral having previously debuted in 1943 on *The Adventures of Superman* radio drama. It made its four-color debut in 1949's *Superman* #61, where it was colored red, the same as in this origin story rehash.

The Kents' names had been finally established as Jonathan and Martha in other comics in the previous few months, and Jonathan is reiterated here, even if Martha isn't called by name. Jor-El and Lara remain the same, but there is an interesting detail revealed that there was room in Kal-El's rocket for his mother, yet she chose to stay with her husband on the dying planet. I don't think Lara won Mother of the Year back then for that choice. Of further note, Clark's time as Superboy does get mentioned here, by a dying Jonathan urging his son to continue as the man in the same way he behaved as the boy.

Speaking of Superboy, it could be argued at this point that all his stories and the titles he starred in are de facto origin stories of Superman. However, the early adventures of young Clark Kent were, at least in the first few years, no different than the tales of his older self. The teenager was even a reporter for his school newspaper. He protected the weak and stood up for what was right, but also seemed inherently good as Ma and Pa Kent only sporadically appeared to mainly praise his altruism. He apparently had already learned the lessons of his foster parents by the time he took up the mantle of Teen of Steel.

Eventually, there are details about the early life of Clark Kent that we get throughout the adventures of Superboy, things like his predilection for relationships with people with the initials L.L. (Lana Lang, Lori Lemaris, Lex Luthor, and Lois Lane, among many others), the origin of the animosity between Superman and Lex Luthor, the introduction of Krypto the Superdog, the continual guidance from Jonathan and Martha, adventures in the far-future with the Legion of Superheroes (a team of youths inspired by his exploits), and many other connected threads revealed throughout the years. However, we are choosing to focus on the man and the specific times in the comics that his origin was retold and the changes therein. Even though elements from the Superboy stories are incorporated into the origin story of Superman, continuity wasn't always the best between the two characters, although that would be addressed and somewhat repaired in the next Great Era of Comic Books.

The Silver Age

The Silver Age of Comics does not have a distinct starting point for Superman. In the early 1950s, superhero comics and stories suffered a sharp decline in popularity. Many characters disappeared from the newsstands, replaced by science fiction and fantasy comics. This was not the case for Superman, however, as National Comics simply applied the new tone to their most popular character's stories. Campiness reigned supreme, Superman's powers became godlike and there seemed to be new Kryptonian survivors popping up left and right. Additionally, Superman was everywhere, including a popular television series that helped ensure that everyone not only knew the character, but what his origin was.

Superman #146 was the only full-length Silver Age depiction of the Man of Steel's origin story. In "The Story of Superman's Life!" writer Otto Binder and artist Al Plastino give us the most detailed telling of Kal-El's beginnings to date. From the mid-1940s through the late 1950s, Superman appeared in a radio show as well as a television series, both of which were titled *The Adventures of Superman* (although the TV show dropped the "*The*"). Both programs had opening dialogue that briefly recounted Superman's origin and abilities. It was likely felt that the comics could just get on with the stories without having to recount the origin.

This time around, Krypton is depicted as even more futuristic and advanced than Earth, with weather-control technology and metal-eating zoo animals and robots made to perform most menial tasks. And yet, for all their intelligence and forward-thinking, they still refuse to believe Jor-El's grave pronouncements that their planet is in peril of imminent demise. Once again, their best scientist must send his infant son away in a rocket mere moments before the planet's destruction. We are privy to an early rocket test with Krypto, the result of which is the poor dog's prototype rocket being knocked off course, explaining why he doesn't make it to Earth until Kal becomes Superboy. Jor-El and Lara still have no choice other than to send baby Kal away on another rocket as Krypton explodes, this time followed by the mineral Kryptonite.

Arriving on Earth, the extraterrestrial toddler is ejected from his self-destructing rocket just before he is found by Jonathan and Martha Kent, who leave him at an orphanage before later returning to adopt him. His various superpowers (invincibility, super-strength, super-breath, super-speed, x-ray vision, among many others) manifest themselves from the get-go. However, his powers are more fully explained here, with his ability to fly attributed to Earth's lower gravity and, for the first time in an origin story, the rest of his super-abilities are explained as a result of Earth's yellow sun (Krypton having had a red sun).

The rest of the story follows the familiar path of Clark becoming Superboy in Smallville, helping the helpless all the while going to great lengths to keep that nosy Lana Lang from discovering his secret identity, much like he would have to do later in Metropolis with that nosy Lois Lane. We do get an explanation of why Clark wears glasses other than a weak attempt to look different than Superman. When his heat vision manifests itself, he has a difficult time controlling it. To keep from accidentally harming anyone, he fashions eyewear using glass from the rocket ship that brought him to Earth. The blankets he was wrapped in also provide the material for his indestructible costume (yay for Kryptonian textiles).

Once again, the Kents die, motivating Clark to leave Smallville for Metropolis. He does return later to also leave as Superboy (got to protect that secret identity!), but not before baking a giant super-cake big enough for everyone in town to get a piece. Although, it turns out that most save the piece as a souvenir.

An interesting added detail shows the adult Superman being granted honorary citizenship in all the countries of the United Nations, to which Supes is humbly honored, yet reaffirms his loyalty to the United States. Today it seems like an odd detail to include, but by then he was well-known for fighting for Truth, Justice, and the American Way. This origin tale ends with the more familiar refrain of "is it a bird? A plane...a rocket? No...it's Superman!"

The Bronze Age

Remember earlier when things got a little complicated with Superman's origin and the inconsistent naming of not only Kal's Kryptonian parents, but also the Kents and the inconsistencies between the stories of Superboy and the adventures of Superman? Well, the Bronze Age of Comic Books had a nifty little explanation for that. The Silver Age had brought back many superheroes that had not been published for a few years, this time with new origins and revamped costumes. To explain what that meant for the previous versions of those characters, the Flash had established a parallel Earth, dubbed Earth-Two, as the home of all the Golden Age stories and characters, with the modern-day versions existing on Earth-One (yes, the naming really should have been the other way around as the Golden Age came first, but that's an argument for another book).

As Superman never faded away or ceased publication this distinction didn't seem to apply to him or was at least trickier to define. However, it was finally established that Kal-L, son of Jor-L and Lara-L, adopted by Jon and Mary Kent, who didn't start his crime-fighting career until he was an adult reporter for the Daily Star, was the Earth-Two version of Superman. It was still a bit confusing as to what stories applied to which version of Superman, but it did provide writers with a convenient way to make sense of it all, at least somewhat. As more alternate realities were established it's logical to deduce that there would also be an Earth were baby Kal-El was taken in by Eben and Sarah Kent, although this was never established.

To catch people up on the main Superman's origin, DC Comics published "The Origin of Superman!" written by E. Nelson Bridwell with artists Carmine Infantino, Curt Swan, and Murphy Anderson in the pages of 1973's oversize *Amazing World of Superman* magazine. This re-telling is fairly by-the-numbers, but at least includes Superboy in the recounting.

The story's ending is nearly identical to the one depicted in *Superman* #146, as is much of the rest of it. Worth noting, this time Superman readily accepts his honorary citizenship in all the U. N. nations without feeling the need to point out his loyalty to the U.S. It's a small but telling distinction in shifting Superman to being a hero for the entire world. The final dialog from the previous comic is also re-written to one often repeated since the 1950s television show: "Look! Up in the sky! It's a bird! It's a plane! It's Superman!"

Six years later, to celebrate five hundred issues of *Action Comics*, and likely to capitalize on the huge success of the then-recent *Superman* theatrical film, Superman's origin was again recounted, detailing all of the facets of Superman continuity to that point. Writer Martin Pasko and artists Curt Swan and Frank Chiaramonte open "The Life Story of Superman" with a prologue very familiar to a generation of fans:

"Faster than a speeding bullet… More powerful than a locomotive… Able to leap tall buildings in a single bound… Look! Up in the sky! It's a bird! It's a plane! It's Superman!"

The story itself concerns the opening of the Superman pavilion at the Metropolis World Fair with the Man of Steel himself giving patrons an exclusive tour of the building and his life. Well, mostly. There are obviously parts that he must keep to himself and only reveal to the readers via internal monologue. The origin itself is, much like in *Amazing World of Superman*, an almost panel for panel retelling of *Superman* #146, albeit redrawn.

Details that had been added to the mythos over the years are included here, such as the Phantom Zone, Supergirl, the various types of Kryptonite, the Fortress of Solitude, and Superman's rogue's gallery consisting of the Toyman, the Parasite, Lex Luthor, and Brainiac. While they don't necessarily contribute to his origin, per se, it does encapsulate the full story of Superman. All of this is within the framework of an overarching plot by Lex Luthor to capture Superman's memories and persona within a clone and use that to discredit the Metropolis Marvel. It's a plot that is as odd as it sounds and ultimately fails.

There were two other miniseries published towards the end of the 1970s that are worth noting. *World of Krypton* and *Krypton Chronicles* work more as the origin of Jor-El than anything else. They both basically outline the lineage of the El family going back many generations. While they don't directly impact the later story of Superman himself, they definitely show us that heroism and doing the right thing are not just a product of his upbringing on Earth.

The Modern Age

And then *Crisis on Infinite Earths* happened, and everything known about Superman was wiped away. No, really! DC Comics had decided that their comic book universes had become way too complicated, and their characters diluted by fifty years of confusing continuity and multiple iterations across multiple Earths, so they published a year-long maxiseries that literally destroyed their vast multiverse and refashioned it as a single continuum. As a result, all their characters were rebooted and started fresh, at least most of them. Regarding Superman, DC Comics brought in a lifelong fan to reimagine the character as if he was being created for the first time in 1986.

John Byrne kicked off the new, rebooted era of Superman with a six-issue bi-weekly series entitled *The Man of Steel*. Byrne started from scratch, stripping away the barnacles of fifty years of continuity, and taking the beginnings of the Man of Tomorrow back to the basics. No more Superboy, no more Krypto, no more other survivors of Krypton, no more alternate Earth doppelgangers. Think of this restart as if Superman had just been created and was being published for the first time, albeit in 1986. This new mini-series even led to a new *Superman* #1!

OK, so, before we dive into the details, there was about a year gap between the end of *Crisis* and the start of *The Man of Steel*. During this time, DC started publishing a series called *Secret Origins* which sought to be the definitive origin stories of their characters for this new, post-*Crisis* continuity. And, of course, for the first issue it seemed reasonable that they would start with the character that started everything. Yes, indeed, *Secret Origin* #1 featured the origin of none other than Superman...the Golden Age Superman.

For some unfathomable reason, they decided to start the new era of simplified continuity by reminding everyone that there used to be another Superman and to talk about his fifty years of existence. Except this wasn't a return of the multiverse and Earth-Two, because right after this that original incarnation of the character was quickly forgotten and not spoken about for the next twenty years. And, so, DC Comics ensured that the "new origin" of Superman that followed a few months later would not be confusing at all...

Anyway, back to basics with Byrne. As stated, this was a complete rebuilding of Superman's origin from the ground up. A lot of characters and plot points that had been added to the story over the last few decades were jettisoned in favor of a more streamlined, cohesive story that would set the tone for the new, post-*Crisis* Man of Tomorrow. Each of the six issues focused on a particular aspect of the origin and managed to clearly define this new canon. It also managed to adhere to the basics of the earlier origin story while collecting the disparate details that had originally been ill-defined.

We start where it always begins, on Krypton in its final days. However, unlike the fantastical retro sci-fi world of yore, this Krypton is much more akin to the stark, sterile environment depicted in the 1978 motion picture. Jor-El and Lara are part of a society so advanced that they've lost the need and desire for human connection, where procreation was a result of mixing DNA in birthing matrices with the resulting babies raised and tutored by robots. As a result, Kal-El is sent to Earth as a fetus, his birthing vessel attached to an experimental warp engine. He gestates during the trip and is actually born once the device lands on Earth, effectively having him born an American (giving more reason and weight to the credo "for truth, justice, and the American way!").

He is again fated to be found by Jonathan and Martha Kent outside of Smallville, but another tweak, and a convenient blizzard, allows them to pass him off as their own child instead of leaving him anonymously at an orphanage and later adopting him. Even Clark believes that he is the Kents' birthchild and doesn't learn the truth until he's a senior in high school. His powers manifest themselves slowly as a child, due to Earth's yellow sun. Pa Kent finally tells him the story of finding him in a rocket, but even then, they think it is a terrestrial rocket and not sent from a distant world. That revelation would come later.

Another important realignment of the lore is that Ma and Pa Kent don't die as a motivation for Clark to leave for Metropolis and become a superhero. They survive this origin story but are still a catalyst for him to use his powers to help the helpless and actually help him devise his Superman identity. Which is another small distinction; this origin story clearly defines Superman as the "disguise" and Clark Kent as who he is. Superman also never states that he has an alter-ego which removes the annoyance of Lana Lang and Lois Lane obsessively trying to discover it or attempting to prove that Clark is Superman. Everyone just assumes that Superman is always who he is. And while this story is heavily influenced by the feature film series, Byrne's depiction of Clark as an adult leans heavily on how he was depicted in the 1950s George Reeves TV series.

The second issue builds out a stronger story for Lois Lane, greatly distancing her from the typical damsel in distress and painting her more as a strong, independent woman and a tenacious, if impulsive, investigative journalist. This seems to also be borrowed from the 1978 movie, but also takes inspiration from the 1950s television series. Much like this mini-series would define who Superman was for the next few decades, this issue did likewise for Lois Lane going forward. She would no longer be a romantic foil and a pawn for Superman's villains (for the most part), but a singular character in her own right.

Issue three gives us the origin of the World's Finest team, specifically the first interaction between Superman and Batman. Being the most popular characters appearing in National Periodical's comic books in the 1940s, it was inevitable back then that the two would be featured together. They originally appeared in separate stories in the anthology series *World's Best Comics* (later retitled *World's Finest*) before regularly teaming up and becoming best friends. Things are portrayed very differently in *The Man of Steel* as their methods of fighting crime are almost diametrically opposed and though they part with a mutual respect, they are far from being the super-friends they had been in the previous continuity.

The next issue brings Lex Luthor into the fold, but, like the other characters and elements in this series so far, in an updated way. Previously, Luthor had been portrayed as a genius scientist, mostly bent on power and later became obsessed with destroying the alien Superman. This latter animosity was subsequently explained by an incident in Smallville when Superboy accidentally ruined one of Luthor's experiments and caused him to lose his hair (it really was a simpler time back then).

In this revised origin story, Luthor gets perhaps the most drastic alteration of all as he is now a billionaire businessman and the most powerful person in Metropolis. He effectively runs the city and, to make him even more slimy, has been lusting after Lois Lane. His latest scheme involves provoking a terrorist attack on one of his parties, which is thwarted by Superman, as basically a job interview to put the Man of Steel on his payroll. Supes dutifully declines and an incensed mayor, who is in attendance, has Luthor arrested for putting people in danger. Lex views this as an affront to his control of the city perpetrated by Superman and vows to destroy the do-gooder.

Two years story-wise and one issue later, in a very distinct call-back to *Action Comics* #500, Luthor tries to make good on that threat by cloning his new nemesis so that he might have his own super-soldier. Unfortunately, the process was predicated on cloning a human and this is where Lex discovers that Superman isn't from this planet as the resultant duplicate is bizarrely faulty and oh-so monstrous. This issue also serves to flesh out the supporting characters a bit more as we get further insight into Perry White and Jimmy Olsen.

All this leads into a final issue where Clark himself discovers his extraterrestrial origins with the resultant existential crisis causing him to re-examine his life in this new context while recommitting to his role as a champion of all of humanity. It's a wonderful sequence that really defines who Superman is to himself and the reader. It acknowledges his American citizenship while also making it clear that his mission involves the entire world.

And that was the status quo for a while, a pared-down, stripped-down, back to basics Superman. Except that once John Byrne left the Superman titles after two years, subsequent writers began finding ways to add back in excised pre-*Crisis* elements of the mythos. Supergirl, Superboy, and Krypto had all been introduced, or re-introduced, in some form or another, albeit not as the versions fondly remembered. Supergirl was now a protoplasmic synthetic lifeform from another dimension that merged with an Earth girl. Superboy was an escaped clone grown from the combined DNA of Lex Luthor and Kal-El. And Krypto was actually from Krypton, but one from an imaginary universe (there were also two other regular Earth pups called Krypto over the years as well).

Other, minor elements were woven in, too, so much so that DC decided in 2003 to spell out everything in a brand-new limited series origin tale. Written by Mark Waid, with artwork by Leinil Francis Yu and Gerry Alanguilan, *Superman: Birthright* updates *The Man of Steel* series in a number of ways over twelve issues. This was also published during a time where comic book stories took their time to unfold, almost in sharp contrast to six decades earlier when an origin story was told rapid-fire style in a handful of panels.

As with all the origins of Superman thus far, this one begins on Krypton with Jor-El and Lara. This Krypton harkens back to the retro sci-fi vibe of the Silver Age and eschews the sterile, cold perfection of Byrne's depiction. As they are readying baby Kal for his historic rocket trip, the Els mourn the loss of their society's achievements, and also never know if their son will reach his destination (foreshadowing alert!).

From there, the story basically tells a parallel tale of Clark Kent's burgeoning journalistic career and his emergence as the Superman of Metropolis. Very little is revealed about Clark's younger years other than a couple of key moments. The first involves budding freelance reporter Kent learning an abject lesson in becoming personally invested in a story while also learning the limits of using his superabilities to solve people's problems for them. The other brings back a Silver Age element to Clark Kent's younger years in Smallville.

In the first case, Clark Kent, a young freelance reporter, is in West Africa to interview and write a story on a political leader and human rights activist, Kobe Asuru. Asuru's opposition wants to permanently silence the activist and, although Clark has been protecting Asuru, eventually succeeds in assassinating him. Clark learns that he can't be in two places at once as a result, but Asuru's sister, Abena, vows to continue his cause. Abena witnesses Clark using his powers to uncover the assassination plot but promises to keep his secret. Through Abena, Clark learns how inspiring righteous words and actions can be.

In the second case, *Birthright* re-establishes that Lex Luthor lived in Smallville for a time and met high school student Clark Kent then. *Birthright*'s depiction of Luthor returns him to being a genius scientist, albeit one bent on gaining power. He reveals to his only friend, Clark Kent, that he has created a sub-space communicator and intends to use it to open a gateway to another planet. He's recently found an extraterrestrial meteor to power the device which turns out to be, you guessed it, Kryptonite. Of course, the device overloads causing a fire that burns off Lex's hair and kills a passed-out-drunk Lionel Luther.

Speaking of Luthor's sub-space communicator, it plays a major part in the "present day" portion of the story as Lex does manage to get a connection to Krypton and uses the images he sees to construct a fake alien invasion from Supes' home planet in order to turn public opinion against his foe. He manages to create a more direct link to Krypton moments before its destruction that gives Jor-El and Lara (and baby Kal!) front-row seats to Superman foiling Luthor's plans. As the connection between worlds collapses, Kal is able to let his parents know that he made the journey they're about to send him on safely.

Also, for the first time in the comics, we get a Kryptonian origin for the "S" symbol on Superman's costume. Everyone just assumed that it stood for Superman. The Christopher Reeve film offered that it was the crest for the House of El. Turns out that it is a symbol for hope and a better tomorrow. This is used in the film *Man of Steel* and continues as part of the Superman lore going forward. *Birthright* also keeps the Kents alive and depicts them as younger, similar to how they were portrayed in the TV series *Smallville*.

Interestingly, *Birthright* was originally published with the intention of being an out-of-continuity retelling of the Man of Steel's origin. However, mid-way through its run the canon-stamp-of-approval was applied, and it became the official origin of Superman, at least for a few years. Because, of course, DC Comics can't help but shake up the status quo every few years with a Crisis or whatnot.

In 2005, *Infinite Crisis* celebrated the twentieth anniversary of the original *Crisis on Infinite Earths*. However, instead of leveling the decks and establishing a new status quo, this new Crisis instead returned a lot of continuity, characters, and plot points that had originally been removed from the company's history. A highlight of all of this was the return of the Golden Age Superman, Kal-L of Earth-Two. Unfortunately, he made the ultimate sacrifice to ensure the survival of the newly restored multiverse.

It was not immediately clear if this latest Earths-shattering event had changed or altered Superman in any way. DC editorial seemed to want to have any new or returning elements unfold over time within the Superman titles themselves. However, this only served to sow confusion, both among fans and creators involved in the books, as to what was and wasn't considered canon.

DC finally relented and enlisted Geoff Johns and Gary Frank to finally detail what was to be billed at the time as the definitive origin of Superman. Johns and Frank did so in a new six-issue 2009 mini-series entitled *Superman: Secret Origin.*

The most striking thing about *Secret Origin* is, contrary to every other retelling of Superman's origin, it does not begin on Krypton. In fact, there are no scenes on the doomed planet and the only glimpse we get of Jor-El and Lara are holographic projections from Kal's rocket ship.

Instead, the story begins with a teenaged Clark discovering his powers and deciding that he wants to use them to help people. From that, for the first time in over twenty years, Clark Kent becomes a costumed Superboy and starts his career in Smallville. Well, not fully, as he operates in secret and hides his presence from those he helps. This is mainly because he's embarrassed about his super-suit. Yes, he gets over that.

This series also reestablishes his connection to the Legion of Superheroes, which was retconned away during *Crisis on Infinite Earths.* This was somewhat hinted at in a post-*Infinite Crisis* storyline, "Superman and the Legion of Superheroes," also by Geoff Johns and Gary Frank. The earlier storyline contributed to canon-confusion regarding the Man of Steel that eventually necessitated this series. It's like Johns deliberately sowed confusion to get himself further work. I'm sure that wasn't the case, though. Mostly sure.

At any rate, *Secret Origin* returned a lot of elements that John Byrne's *Man of Steel* did away with two decades earlier. Clark as Superboy was back, Krypto arrived shortly after Kal, the Legion members were once again childhood friends of the Teen of Steel, and several other bits and pieces were reestablished. Once again, we had a concrete, well-defined complete origin of Superman to carry us forward and forever be unchanged.

And then, around a year later, all of that was wiped away as

DC Comics rebooted their entire line...again. Thanks to the events of *Flashpoint*, this was an even bigger deal than *Crisis on Infinite Earths*. All DC comics were canceled, and everything was restarted with new number one issues. Ok, not *completely* rebooted. There were some storylines that remained intact, but some were negated and...yes, ok, this was almost as much of a mess as the reboot from the original *Crisis on Infinite Earths*.

What's pertinent to us is that many of the Silver Age trappings that *Secret Origin* brought back were once again done away with. Again. A lot of this wasn't made clear as it would be a couple of years before there was an origin retell for the Man of Steel. The *Superman* title told stories of the "present-day" Kal-El with a Kryptonian-armor style of super-suit only a few years into his career, both as crime-fighter and crime reporter. *Action Comics* gave us a Clark Kent before he became widely known as the Metropolis Marvel. While not quite a super-boy, this young adult version was clad in a t-shirt with the familiar shield emblazoned on it, jeans, and combat boots.

A few years into the "New 52," writer Greg Pak and artist Lee Weeks presented a very stripped-down beginning for Superman, yet a very familiar one, in a new volume of *Secret Origins*. Krypton was depicted as a more updated sci-fi utopia, akin to how it eventually looked in the *Man of Steel* film. Again, baby Kal is rocketed away moments before the planet is destroyed, crashes on Earth, and is found and adopted by the Kents. They meet a tragic end in his youth, which spurs him to quietly start using his powers for good.

And then, five years after it revitalized the entire DC Comics line for a new generation, the "New 52" initiative came to an unceremonious end. Basically, the previous reality wasn't quite removed from existence and elements of it were causing havoc in the new timeline. Chief among these was the *Superman: Secret Origin* version of Clark Kent and Lois Lane who had been living their lives together in seclusion this whole time. They'd also managed to have a son, Jon Kent, who was definitely a chip off his father's Kryptonian-powered block.

Eventually, the two Supermen teamed-up to fight a major threat, giving DC the ability to kill a Superman again. Through a further convoluted storyline, Supes was able to cause the two realities to merge, thus bringing back the previous continuity while retaining the "New 52" elements that the publisher deemed worth keeping. Typing that all out makes it sound pretty absurd and almost feels like someone, somewhere was using reality-warping abilities to deliberately remake the DC Universe in general, and Superman in particular, over again every few years. Turns out, someone was.

While ostensibly a sequel to the 1986 *Watchmen* maxi-series, the 2018 *Doomsday Clock* reveals what, or who, was behind the complete universal reboot following *Flashpoint*. That might seem like a really nonsensical statement, but it is also true. Written by Geoff Johns and drawn by Gary Frank (remember those two?), this story offered some revelations about the nature of the DC Comics universe.

Following the events of the *Watchmen* series, Doctor Manhattan discovered the DC Universe. More importantly, he discovered that the universe was part of a metaverse and constantly in flux. Important to us, he further discovered that Superman was the focal point of this metaverse and that outside forces have been causing his arrival on Earth to shift forward in time, the byproduct of which have been the continual Crises-caused reboots. Manhattan himself caused the reboot that resulted from *Flashpoint*, mainly to see what would happen and to see if he could determine the cause of all these changes.

In the end, Doctor Manhattan undoes the changes he made to the DC Universe, resulting in the events that merged the timelines, but is unable to determine who or what the outside manipulation is stemming from. There are a subsequent string of crossover events and storylines that kind of get into that, but at least for the time being, we're back to the *Superman: Secret Origin* continuity for Superman, although that isn't completely clear either.

Taking a breather from all the continual reboots and multiversal shenanigans, DC Comics decided to reboot the main *Superman* title with a new number one issue with writer Brian Michael Bendis and penciller Ivan Reis. Sounds like a good excuse to retell Supes' origin, right? You know it! This time we got a spiritual sequel to Byrne's 1986 re-do in a weekly series with the same title, *The Man of Steel*.

Why a sequel only in spirit? Well, the goal of this 2018 miniseries was not to reinvent the Metropolis Marvel for a whole new generation. Instead, Bendis set up the stories he planned to tell in *Action Comics* and the new *Superman* title. So, why is this even mentioned in regard to Superman's origin? Because it introduces a key factor to said origin that is a pretty big doozy.

As introduced in this new miniseries and expanded upon in the first year and a half of the new *Superman* series, the destruction of Krypton was not necessarily a naturally-occurring phenomenon. Years before he sent his son to Earth, Jor-El had created a monstrous super-soldier that eventually grew to hate his creator and all his people. Rogol Zaar swore to eradicate all Kryptonians and seems to have caused the explosion that destroyed the planet, or he at least accelerated the process.

Decades later, Zaar learned about the bottle city of Kandor and followed it to Earth. He managed to destroy the miniaturized city and all who resided within before finally being stopped by Superman, Supergirl, Jon Kent, and Krypto. Oh, and Jor-El was still alive in present day, thanks to Dr. Manhattan snatching him between the seconds of Kal-El's rocket leaving Krypton and the planet going *kablam* and depositing him on Earth. And then Superman revealed his secret identity to the world.

There was a lot going on in the first couple of years of *Superman* Volume Five. While there wasn't a full retelling of the Man of Steel's origin during that time, a couple of key elements were obviously altered and given a different perspective. It remains to be seen if these new elements will survive either the next re-telling of the origin story or the next universal reboot.

The Future: How It's Going

That brings us up to date on the telling of Superman's origin in the mainstream DC Comics universe. As you can see, it has changed, evolved, *de-evolved*, and looped back around over the last several decades. This doesn't even consider the number of Elseworlds, alternate universe, and reimagined takes on Superman's story that exist in the pages of various comic book series. Most are variations on a theme, with Kal-El's rocket landing in various places other than Smallville, Kansas. Some are completely rewritten, and some are very bizarre.

As this is being written, there is yet another DC Universe shattering event going on, *Dark Crisis on Infinite Earths*, a new sequel to the original *Crisis*, which promises to restore the infinite multiverse. You will know by the time you are reading this whether this remains a full accounting of Superman's fluid origin or if there needs to be a revision. But, hey, don't worry. If it is all getting rebooted once again it will likely get changed once more in a few years!

Long may comic books continue to be published and long may they continue to tell us the origin story of the Man of Tomorrow, the Man of Steel, the Last Son of Krypton—Superman!

Joseph Dilworth Jr. is a long-time internet writer, essaying his opinions about pop culture at places such as *Long Island Pulse Magazine* and his own website, Pop Culture Zoo (now called What Joe Writes). Joe is currently the co-host of The Flickcast podcast, as well as co-host of Highlander Heart and a writer and editor for several pop culture books published by the Sequart Organization. He has an unhealthy obsession with obscure 70s and 80s television. Joe resides in the Pacific Northwest where he spends time with his family, 3D printing, brewing mead, writing, reading, and still spouting his opinions to whoever will listen. Just be warned: never, ever feed him after midnight. Also: Be kind, rewind.

BATMAN

First Appearance: Detective Comics #27, March 30th 1939

The Re-Told Legend of Batman: Who He Is and All of the Ways He Came to Be

By Michael Bailey

Batman has one of the best superhero origin stories of all time. This is no mere opinion. It is an objective fact. The backbone of that origin is simple, effective, and emotionally connects the audience to the character. It's so good that the basic framework of the origin would be a constant since it was revealed in 1939.

The specifics, though? The details? The little bits and bobs that flesh out the backstory? Those are less permanent. They can be added, taken away, put back, or forgotten by the fickle nature of a changing creative, editorial, or executive regime. It's those details that are worth examining. What were those changes? Why did they occur? Why were certain details put back in later? How did the changes in the people responsible for crafting Batman's stories affect his origin? All of those questions and more are worth examining because they say as much about the comic book medium and the company that publishes Batman as they do about Batman himself.

Quick note before we get into this: For the purposes of this essay the term "origin" will be defined as anything that happened before Bruce Wayne suited up for the first time. Even if those events are brought to light or discovered later in his career. As long as those revelations have something to do with Bruce deciding that becoming a bat to put fear into the hearts of a superstitious and cowardly lot was the way to go to become a crime fighter, they are on the table and fair game. I felt that this was an important distinction to make because a lot of what we think of as being essential to Batman's origin came much later in his publishing history.

Sound good?

All right. Let's begin.

The Golden Age or You Know, We Might Want to Tell People Why This Guy Dresses Up as a Bat

Batman's first appearance in *Detective Comics* #27 should rank as one of the all-time best first appearances in superhero comics. "The Case of the Chemical Syndicate" is a fantastic story that establishes the Bat-Man (the hyphen was a thing in his first few appearances) as a fearsome figure that preys on criminals and works outside of the law. We also learn that this Bat-Man is actually socialite Bruce Wayne in a reveal that must have been shocking to the kids and adults reading the story for the first time in 1939.

The thing is that while the story gets a lot done in its six pages, it does not reveal why Bruce has become a masked vigilante. *Detective Comics* #28 doesn't mention it either. Issues #29 through #32 likewise fail to reveal this important piece of information. It isn't until *Detective Comics* #33, in a story commonly referred to as "Batman Wars Against the Dirigible of Doom," his backstory is revealed and it does not, as the story title suggests, involve an airship.

It doesn't even take up two full pages of that story.

It's almost like the people writing, drawing, and publishing these Batman stories got to his seventh appearance and said, "Wait, we haven't revealed his backstory yet. People might be curious about that, but, at the same time, we have this exciting story about Batman fighting against someone in a dirigible and we don't want to mess with that because the kids love dirigibles, so slap it on the first two pages and move on. In fact, it will only get the bottom third of that first page. This airship story is just too important to interrupt."

I'm sure the discussion between Vincent Sullivan (the then-editor of *Detective Comics*), Bill Finger (the writer of the origin part of the story and co-creator of Batman), and Bob Kane (the artist on that story and co-creator of Batman) was more nuanced than that, but the origin piece certainly feels like an afterthought.

This isn't surprising when you compare Batman to other adventure strips of the time. While many did include an origin in the character's first appearance just as many others simply tell an adventure about the character and introduce elements on the fly. So, not having Batman's backstory spelled out in his appearance wasn't common, it wasn't uncommon either.

Finger and Kane get a lot done with the origin in the limited space they have. All of the basics are laid out. Fifteen years ago, young Bruce Wayne was walking with his parents when a gunman approached. The gunman demands their valuables and when Bruce's father resists the gunman shoots him. He shoots Bruce's mother as well when she starts screaming. Bruce makes a solemn vow that he will dedicate his life to avenging his parents and as he grows into manhood, he trains his body and his mind. Years later Bruce sits in his study and muses on how he has nearly everything he needs to wage his war, but something is missing. A bat flies into the window, Bruce spots it, realizes that the image of that bat was the final piece of his puzzle, and thus is born a weird figure of the night.

The simplicity of the origin is the main reason it works so well. Bruce lost his parents to a violent act and instead of living the life of a wealthy socialite, which he could have easily done, he honored the memory of his mother and father by fighting the type of people that took them from him. His oath read as, "And I swear by the spirits of my parents to avenge their deaths by spending the rest of my life warring on all criminals."

Note that the oath mentions nothing about finding the man that killed his mother and father. This is an important distinction. There is a big difference between payback and having the deep desire to make sure that what happened to you doesn't happen to everyone else. Also, becoming the Bat-Man to find one criminal is limiting in terms of an ongoing strip. There is nothing to say that Bat-Man can't go on fighting muggers, killers, and thieves after finding the man that killed his parents, but that isn't how the oath was originally worded.

Outside of reprinting that one and a half pages in *Batman* #1 (Spring 1940) the Batman's background was largely ignored in favor of telling stories about his ongoing adventures. That changed in the pages of *Batman* #47 (June/July 1948). By this point Batman had one story per issue in the pages of *Detective Comics*, another story per issue in *World's Finest Comics*, and up to three stories in *Batman*. This meant there needed to be more grist for the mills, so expanding on the origin was now on the table. The result? "The Origin of Batman," written by Bill Finger with art by Bob Kane, which was the third story in *Batman* #47.

The story begins with Batman and Robin happening upon an accident involving a truck that was used to smuggle wanted criminals across state lines. Batman is given a photograph of the owner of the trucking company and is shocked to realize that the man in the picture, Joe Chill, is also the man that shot his mother and father. This is followed by a retelling of the origin which contained changes that seem subtle but actually represent a paradigm shift in Batman's mission and motivation.

The first change is how the Waynes were killed. In the original telling Martha was shot right after Thomas to keep her from screaming. In this story she dies because her weak heart stopped from the shock of witnessing her husband getting gunned down. Also, young Joe Chill is *freaked out* by the way Bruce glares at him. It legitimately unsettles him. The artwork is trippy here and sells the idea that Bruce's eyes made Chill so uncomfortable that he retreats instead of shooting Bruce. Finally, the location and verbiage of the oath is altered. In this telling, Bruce makes his oath not at his bedside but at his parents' graves and the wording adds to the scope of his future mission. Young Bruce vows, "I swear I'll dedicate my life and inheritance to bringing your killer to justice…and to fighting all criminals! I swear it!"

While the visual of Bruce staring at Joe Chill is relatively minor, the other two additions actually change the narrative. Martha dying of a heart attack instead of getting shot softens her death. A heart attack is no less deadly, but as a visual it is less gruesome. It is still traumatic for Bruce, but it did begin a minimization of Martha's role in Bruce's path to becoming Batman that continued for the next several decades.

The reason for this particular change is more than likely due to the shift in tone in comic books in general. After World War Two interest in superheroes was on the decline and other genres, such as funny animal characters and westerns, rose in prominence. Batman had been softening as a character even longer than that. Early on the powers that be at Detective Comics, Inc. were shifting the tenor of Batman's stories from gritty, pulp detective tales to more light-hearted, costumed adventures to build a more sustainable brand. Jack Liebowitz (co-owner of Detective Comics, Inc.) and Whitney Ellsworth (successor to Vin Sullivan as editor of *Detective Comics* and *Batman*) created a code of conduct for their characters. Liebowitz wanted to build a children's entertainment empire and Batman's early actions, such as kicking a man and breaking his neck or using a machine gun to take down giant monster men created by Dr. Hugo Strange did not help in that endeavor.

Thomas being shot and killed was acceptable. Martha being likewise shot and killed was probably a bridge too far.

It also made her death seem less important to Bruce, which is apparent at the end of the story when Bruce closes the case on the death of Thomas Wayne. Martha is not mentioned. Even though the death of her husband was what ultimately killed Martha, her passing seems to not be as important in terms of Batman confronting Joe Chill. To be fair, Bruce does mention both his father and mother when he's glaring at Joe Chill and the tombstone at the graveside oath is inscribed with both Thomas and Martha's name, but in the final panel of the story Batman uses his fancy pen to write "Closed" on a page with the header reading, "Murder of Thomas Wayne."

The slight change to the oath likewise shifted Batman's basic motivations. The addition of bringing the killer of his parents to justice changed why he does what he does, even if it was included because Batman was confronting that killer in this story. It could be argued that Batman is an unreliable narrator considering the revised death of the Waynes is a flashback in Batman's own mind. He could be misremembering the events surrounding his parents' death. Maybe his original oath didn't contain anything about Thomas or Martha but now that he is confronted with their killer it was suddenly there all along.

Either way, it added an element of vengeance to his overall mission. It didn't detract from his reason to be and while there was a moment in the story where Batman was ready to give up his identity to confront Chill when the story ended Bruce is still fighting crime as Batman. This case merely provided some closure for him.

More Rooms Are Added To The Manor or Where Did He Get That Wonderful Costume?

Two stories published within a year of each other added more to Batman's backstory. The tales had several things in common. They both featured Batman and Robin watching home movies on the cover. They both dealt with where the idea for the costumes for both Batman and Robin came from. They also both added elements to how and why Batman became Batman in the first place.

The first story was "When Batman was Robin," which appeared in *Detective Comics* #226 (December 1955). After receiving a package containing a Robin costume Batman is forced to tell his sidekick about a terrible mistake he made long ago that could endanger both of their careers. The Robin costume was worn by Bruce when he was in his teens to conceal his identity when he approached his idol Harvey Harris to train him to be a detective. The overall plot is gimmicky, but most of Batman's stories in the 1950's were gimmicky and the idea that Batman took the name Robin at some point fit right into that era.

The main focus of this story was to reveal how Batman became the world's greatest detective. Even though he only shared one adventure with Harvey Harris, this is the foundation of Batman's sleuthing abilities. Harris taught Bruce to be observant and showed him the basics of working a case. While Harvey is not a mentor that sticks around, he is important enough that their adventure was still fresh in Batman's mind.

On a more subtle level this story also showed the formation of Bruce taking on a secret identity both in terms of creating that identity and protecting it. While it is Harris that gave Bruce the name Robin, Bruce was the one that put the costume together. There is also a mental sparring match through the course of the story where Harris tries to figure out who this masked teenager is and Bruce tries to not let any details slip that would jeopardize his secret. Harris does figure out that Robin is Bruce, thanks to several slip ups, but this is the genesis of Bruce adopting a disguise to fight crime and it wouldn't be the last identity he came up with.

There is one detail from this story that stands out. Early in the story Bruce is described as being a teenager, but it is also said that the reason he is able to sneak off in a fancy costume to learn how to be a detective is that his parents were abroad for the summer. This means that, in the flashback, they're still alive, which brings up an important question.

Why did Bruce want to become a detective before his parents are killed?

Everything that had been established thus far about the backstory is that Bruce's parents are killed and that led him to train his mind and body to fight crime. This story suggested that he wanted to be a detective before their encounter with Joe Chill, which further suggested that he may have gone into law enforcement whether his parents were killed or not. It doesn't take anything away from his origin. In fact, it may have been why he chose to initially fight outside of the normal system and adopt a costumed identity. His parents' killer was never caught. Law enforcement failed him. He wanted to wage a war on crime, but saw that the normal system was inadequate, so he disguised himself as a bat and while he eventually developed an association with the Gotham City Police, he was never fully part of that system.

This story also threw into doubt the actual timeline of when the Waynes were killed. The original story put their deaths at fifteen years before the events of *Detective Comics* #33, which is more than likely still the first year of Bruce's costumed career. Bruce's age is never expressly given, but he appeared to be in his early to mid-twenties, which meant he was anywhere from eight to twelve years old when he lost his parents. Having Bruce in his teens when they are killed doesn't mitigate what their deaths meant to him, but it did make Batman a little older at the time that "When Batman was Robin" took place.

This is not the last time that the Waynes being alive into Bruce's teens would be mentioned.

The second story that revealed more details into Batman's past was "The First Batman," which was written by Bill Finger with art by Sheldon Moldoff and appeared in *Detective Comics* #235. This story begins with Bruce and Dick finding a costume in the attic that looks very much like the one Bruce wears as Batman. They also discover a diary and a reel of film, which reveals that the costume belonged to Bruce's father. He had worn it to a costume ball where he was taken hostage by criminals who wanted Thomas to patch up their boss Lew Moxon. Moxon had been shot during the course of a bank robbery. Thomas not only took the crooks down but testified against Moxon in court. When Moxon was released, he swore that he would get even and that no one would ever be able to connect it back to him.

The variant costume angle was fun with an interesting design. Finger justified Bruce coming up with a similar design by having him tell Dick that seeing the bat fly into the window must have prodded a subconscious memory of the costume. It didn't take anything away from the iconic shot of the bat flying into the window. It's simply a fun detail meant to get the plot going, but it isn't the most important part of this story.

The important part of this story was revealing that Joey Chill, as

Bill Finger called him here, was hired by Lew Moxon to get revenge on Thomas Wayne for sending him to jail. Bruce even theorized that the reason Moxon had Chill leave Bruce alive was that Bruce could tell the police that someone other than Moxon killed his parents. This meant that the death of the Waynes was not some random street crime. There was something behind their murders that Bruce had been unaware of until he and Dick stumbled across Thomas' costume.

In examining all of this the question then becomes does adding yet another name to the list of people responsible for Bruce becoming Batman water down the overall origin? Revealing that there was someone behind that killer makes the story more complicated than it needs to be. There was nothing wrong with the origin as it was conceived. Why make it some grand conspiracy perpetrated by someone that had a beef with Thomas Wayne?

The answer is the era in which this story was published. 1956 is considered by some to be the start of the Silver Age for DC Comics. Over the next few years, the publisher introduced new versions of discarded characters like Green Lantern, the Flash, Hawkman, and the Atom. The editors and writers also started to play around and expand the mythologies of the characters that managed to stick around. Batman's world expanded with the introduction of Ace the Bat Hound in 1955 and the first Kathy Kane iteration of Batwoman premiering two issues before "The First Batman" was published. An origin for the bat costume and a more complex series of events that led to the death of the Waynes was par for the course and additions and revelations like it would continue into the 1960s.

The idea of Bruce adopting a costumed identity as a teenager was brought out again in "The Origin of the Superman-Batman Team" was a Superboy story written by Jerry Coleman with art by George Papp that appeared in *Adventure Comics* #275. Like "When Batman was Robin," this story featured a young Bruce Wayne putting on a costume, one given to him by Lana Lang to stop an armored tank from robbing a bank. The press dubs him the Flying Fox and he continues to fight crime in Smallville, mainly to help Lana find out Superboy's secret identity.

Why would Bruce do this? To get Lana to go to the junior prom with him.

Silver Age DC. It was a lot of fun.

At times it was goofy, but a lot of fun.

Through the course of the story Superboy makes it his mission to train Bruce in the ways of being a costumed hero because he knows they are destined to be friends as Superman and Batman when they are adults, thanks to a machine that allows him to see into the future. (I promise this makes sense within the context of the story.) Superboy gives Bruce a utility belt at one point and at the end of the adventure he even reveals their future friendship to Bruce, which leads Bruce to abandon the idea of revealing Superboy's identity. The icing on this particular cake is that a flying fox is a type of bat, so even though Superboy removes the memory of him being Clark Kent from Bruce Wayne's mind the idea of becoming a Batman had yet another inspiration, mostly likely from Bruce's subconscious, which seems to get a lot of traffic.

This is another story that threw the timeline of Batman's origin into question. When Bruce is introduced to the other students at Smallville High School the teacher informs them that the Waynes have just moved to town. Thomas and Martha are still alive well into Bruce's teenage years. This wasn't an elementary or middle school. It was a high school and Bruce wanted to go to the junior prom, which meant Bruce is at least sixteen or seventeen during the events of this story. The goal post of when the Waynes were killed kept getting moved further and further into Bruce's teenage years.

Why is this happening?

A good answer to that question would be The Comics Code Authority.

Probably.

The Comics Code Authority was formed in 1954 by a comic industry trade group called The Comics Magazine Association of America. Between a book which demonized comics titled *Seduction of the Innocent*, written by Dr. Frederick Wertham, and The Senate Subcommittee Hearing on Juvenile Delinquency, which was held in

April of 1954, the comics industry was under attack, which led to a group of publishers, including National Periodicals (which was the name DC Comics was known as at the time) formed a self-censoring board to make sure that there wasn't anything objectionable in the comics that they published.

Violence, gore, and sexual activities were at the top of their list of things to avoid in stories, so it made sense that they would downplay how the Waynes were killed. It didn't specifically state that they weren't killed, but that aspect of Batman's origin was sidelined in favor of fun stories where a teenage Bruce Wayne adopted the identity of The Flying Fox and fought crime alongside Superboy.

Silver Gives Way To Bronze or Wait, Crime Alley Wasn't There From The Beginning?

Batman had a rough time of it at the beginning of the Sixties. Sales had fallen to the point that National briefly considered either canceling Batman or killing him off. In 1964 editor Julius Schwartz, the man who pretty much started the Silver Age of Comics, took over the Bat-titles. He brought Batman back to his detective roots and the plots became more about solving the case than traveling in space or turning into a baby. Then came the live-action television series that ran from 1966 to 1968, which was not only a ratings success that was accompanied by a wave of "Batmania," but also brought about a brief spike in the sale of the Batman comics. Unfortunately, when the series ended the books once again fell into a slump.

Between the end of the television series and the start of what is commonly accepted as the Bronze Age era of Batman two more additions were added to Bruce Wayne's history. Both appeared in *Batman* #208 (January/February 1969), which was an 80-Page Giant, a format DC created in the sixties that were (not surprisingly) 80-page comics primarily made up of reprints of older stories. Bucking that trend was issue #208, which contained an original story written by E. Nelson Bridwell with art by Gil Kane titled "The Women in Batman's Life". For the most part that story served as the connective tissue between reprints of tales featuring Catwoman, Vicki Vale, Batwoman, and Batgirl, but it was the final part of the framing story where we met two people from Bruce's past.

The narrator of the story is Mrs. Chilton, who served as the housekeeper of Bruce's Uncle Phillip. Phillip was named as Bruce's guardian, but his career required him to travel quite a bit, so it was up to Mrs. Chilton to look after Bruce. Mrs. Chilton watched Bruce make his graveside vow, which later led her to realize that he was the Batman, a secret which she kept to herself. That wasn't the only secret she kept from Bruce.

Mrs. Chilton is also the mother of Joe Chill.

In addition to that twist ending this story answered the question of who took care of Bruce after his parents died, which, up until this issue, had never been revealed. Bruce went from a small boy (or teenager) right to being an adult. Mrs. Chilton and, to a lesser extent, Uncle Phillip, provided Bruce with a family and from the way Bruce acted towards Mrs. Chilton in the final pages of *Batman* #208 it was a loving family.

Now I know what you may be thinking. "What about Alfred? Wasn't he the man that raised a young Bruce Wayne?"

We'll get to that momentarily.

As Batman entered the 1970s his origin started to revert back to its original form. Part of this had to do with the fact that mainstream comics were changing as a whole. The Comics Code Authority started relaxing their grip on the medium. In February of 1971 Marvel Comics published *Amazing Spider-Man* #96, which began a three-issue storyline involving Spider-Man fighting the Green Goblin, but battling his then arch-enemy wasn't the reason those issues were historical. Stan Lee, the writer of those issues and editor of the Marvel Comics line, was asked by the National Institute on Mental Health to address drug abuse in his comics since they reached a young audience. The Comics Code Authority rejected the story and Lee, annoyed by the fact that there was nothing specifically in the Code about drug use, released the three issues without the Comics Code Authority Seal and then put it back on when the story was over.

This created changes within the Code and the rules began to loosen up and soon National Periodicals was publishing its own drug abuse story in the pages of *Green Lantern/Green Arrow*. Starting with issue #76, *Green Lantern/Green Arrow* (previously just *Green Lantern*) began telling stories that dealt with real world issues, such as corporate greed, the rights of First Nations people, and overpopulation. In issue #85 it was revealed that Speedy, the sidekick of Green Arrow, had a heroin addiction. Suddenly the rather conservative storytelling of National's characters began taking on a more real-world feel.

The writer and artist behind the revamped *Green Lantern/Green Arrow* were Denny O'Neil and Neal Adams. In addition to breathing new life into those heroes, O'Neil and Adams were tasked with getting Batman out of the sales slump he had fallen into. Soon, the titles went from camp to a mix of street level crime and supernatural creature features. O'Neil and Adams produced stories like "The Secret of the Waiting Graves" (published in *Detective Comics* #395), "Paint a Picture of Peril!" (*Detective Comics* #397), and "Challenge of the Man-Bat!" (*Detective Comics* #400). All of these pushed the boundaries of the previous version of the code by dealing with themes of horror and death.

It was in *Batman* #232 (June 1971) where the O'Neil/Adams team dealt with the origin of Batman. In the middle of the story, titled "Daughter of the Demon" O'Neil took a few panels to retell how Bruce became Batman and brought back an element that had been missing for decades.

Martha is once again shot alongside her husband instead of dying of a weak heart.

This was not a minor reversion. It may not have been intentional on the part of O'Neil or Adams but changing the way Martha died not only reflected on how the Batman comics were tripping further into darker territory but also hearkened back to the early days of Batman's existence.

O'Neil also brought back the idea that Bruce was around ten or twelve years old when the Waynes were shot. Gone were the days where they lived into his teen years.

Denny O'Neil contributed two more elements to the backstory in *Detective Comics* #457 (March 1976). O'Neil, along with artist Dick Giordano, produced "There is No Hope in Crime Alley!" a story where Batman makes his yearly pilgrimage on the night his parents were killed. The area where the murders took place is given a name: Park Row, which is a formerly wealthy section of town made up of the rich and the soon-to-be rich. After the death of the Waynes the neighborhood fell on hard times and took on a new name: Crime Alley.

Giving the area where the Waynes died a history and a name was a huge development for Batman. Up until the early Seventies Gotham had been a gleaming city that may have had its share of crime, but you would still want to live there. By suggesting that the area where Thomas and Martha were killed went from being populated by the well to do to criminals and people that weren't able to afford to leave, O'Neil made Batman's mission more important.

It also suggested that the death of the Waynes was not only the turning point for Bruce but for the city itself. An area taking on the name Crime Alley after two prominent citizens were killed there spoke to the need for a Batman in the first place. The police aren't enough. The people needed a hero, and that hero is Batman. Bruce Wayne did his best with his charitable foundations, but Batman was the one on the ground level trying to make the city a safer place.

O'Neil also used "There is No Hope in Crime Alley!" to introduce Dr. Leslie Thompkins. Dr. Thompkins was the woman that was there for Bruce the night his parents were murdered. O'Neil and Giordano showed us that while there were plenty of policemen and reporters on the scene after the Waynes had been killed none of them seemed concerned for young Bruce Wayne. It was Leslie who knelt down and told him to come with her and that she would do what she could for him.

This is another element that had been left out of the previous iterations of the origin. Now the reader knew that there was someone there to comfort Bruce the night his parents were taken away from him and at the end of the story she is there for him again, even though she isn't yet aware that Batman is Bruce Wayne. She shows him that despite the violent world they live in there will always be good people like Leslie Thompkins trying to make it a better place.

The Eighties Part One or Retconning the Night Away

At the dawn of the 1980s a new format popped up in comic books. The mini-series had become a staple for television and starting in 1979 DC began publishing short-run series featuring their big gun characters. Batman got his mini-series in early 1980 in the form of *The Untold Legend of Batman*. This three-issue mini-series was written by Len Wein with art in the first issue by John Byrne and in the second and third issues by Jim Aparo. Wein, like O'Neil, was part of the second wave of comic creators that began working in the late Sixties and part of the first generation that grew up on the comics they were now writing and drawing.

Len started his career at National, but soon moved to Marvel where he worked on *The Incredible Hulk*, *Amazing Spider-Man*, and even helped usher in the new generation of X-Men in *Giant-Sized X-Men* number one. He headed back to National in 1978 and quickly became one of the main writers on the various Batman titles. *Untold Legend of the Batman* came at the tail end of his time working on the Dark Knight as a creator and served as his chance to take the histories of Batman, Robin, Alfred, Commissioner Gordon, and other Bat-related characters and consolidate them into one smooth narrative.

Wein didn't make any major changes to the origin of Batman. It all played out as it had before. Instead, he added to certain elements, like Bruce's time training with Harvey Harris. In the original story Bruce only worked with Harvey on one case. In the re-telling Bruce spends more time with Harris learning not only how to be a detective, but also the finer points of boxing and how to read a fingerprint. Wein did keep the idea that Harris was one of the first to solve the secret of Bruce's double identity. The biggest change was that Bruce's tutelage by Harris took place firmly after the Waynes had been killed. This was the first nail in the coffin of Bruce's parents living into his teenage years.

One original scene that Wein added to Bruce's background took place during his college years. Bruce's narration tells us that he majors in Criminology in college with a minor in Psychology to better understand how the criminal mind worked. It is during his law class that Bruce learns what he considered his greatest lesson. His professor, Amos Rexford, gives the class a scenario where two nineteen-year-old boys steal a car for a joyride. One of them has a change of heart but before he can be let out of the car the driver accidentally strikes an old woman. Professor Rexford asks his class if the boy who wanted out should be charged with murder.

Bruce replies, "Granted, the second boy stole the car, Professor—but he had no part in the accidental death!" Rexford informs Bruce that he would be wrong. The law states that the boy would be just as guilty of complicity as if he had been the one driving. Bruce asks if that is justice and Rexford sternly informs him, "No, Mister Wayne…that's the law!"

After graduation, Bruce stands before his parents' graves and tells them that he cannot become a policeman as he had originally planned. "They're too often hamstrung by the very laws they've sworn to uphold! No, there has to be another way—and I swear I'll find it!" With this small detail, Wein explicitly stated why Bruce chose to work outside of the normal law enforcement channels to honor the oath he made to his parents. By showing that Bruce thought the system itself was hindered by loopholes and inconsistencies Wein showed that becoming a masked crimefighter was the best way for Bruce to bring his parents' killer to justice and to wage war on all criminals.

On a more pedantic front, the true final nail in the coffin of the idea that Bruce's parents lived into his teenage years happened in *World's Finest* #271. In that issue, writer Roy Thomas crafted a story that was meant to explain and streamline all of the various times Superman and Batman met for the first time. In addition to splitting different versions of the characters between the different Earths in the multiverse, Wein also amended one detail from *Adventure Com-*

ics #275 in, of all places, an editor's note.

On page sixteen of that issue, Thomas and artists Rich Buckler and Frank McLaughlin recreated the moment from the original *Adventure Comics* story where the teacher introduced Bruce to the class, complete with the teacher explaining that Bruce had just moved to town with his parents. In a caption at the bottom of the panel, editor Len Wein added, "Actually they were only his guardians; but even teachers make mistakes, right?" Now, it was a minor point, but in the original story it was plainly stated that it was Bruce's parents that brought him to Smallville. More than anything this change smacked more of a then current editor or writer (it is not clear if Wein made the note on his own or if Roy Thomas had asked him to) wanting to tweak a minor piece of continuity because it didn't fit into the current narrative, which was becoming more of a thing at the time.

The Eighties Part Two or It's Frank Miller's World and Batman is Just Living in It

Starting in January of 1985, DC Comics (publisher Jeannette Kahn changed the name of the company from National Periodical to DC Comics soon after she was hired in 1976 in an effort to legitimize the idea of being a comics company) published a twelve-issue maxi-series titled *Crisis on Infinite Earths*. *Crisis* was the brainchild of writer Marv Wolfman and Len Wein and the purpose of the series, outside of celebrating DC's fiftieth birthday, was to do away with the idea that the characters they published existed in a multiverse, which they felt was too confusing for new readers.

After the series ended, DC set about revamping and rebooting several of their biggest characters. Superman and Wonder Woman were given near top-to-bottom makeovers. Batman, on the other hand, didn't. His history was largely untouched and even though his origin would be retold in a four-issue storyline, the main beats that had been there from the beginning remained.

The particulars of that origin were another story and those changes and the entire ethos of Batman that would eventually inspire an entire generation of people that told his stories came at the hands of a writer/artist named Frank Miller.

Frank Miller entered the comics industry in 1978 working as a freelancer for both Marvel and DC Comics. His big break came when he was given the penciling duties on the Marvel series *Daredevil*, which he would soon start writing as well. He took Daredevil back to his more crime noir roots and soon the book became both a commercial and critical success. After *Daredevil*, Miller penciled the Wolverine limited series and then went over to DC and produced a six-issue mini-series titled *Ronin*. It was after his second, shorter run on *Daredevil* that Miller made his mark on Batman.

In March of 1986, DC published the first issue of a four-issue mini-series titled *Batman: The Dark Knight*. It was a story of Batman's future, where Bruce Wayne had given up being the Dark Knight but came back when the pressures of suppressing that side of him combined with a Gotham City that had descended further into chaos caused him to suit up once more. It was a bold story that broke new ground with the character. Not since his first year of publication had Batman been this violent and never had Gotham City been this much of a haven for scum and villainy.

It also broke new ground in terms of how it was originally published and later where most people would eventually read it. Instead of being printed in your standard comic book, the series came out in square-bound books that could be stored on a bookshelf just as easily as in a comic box. When the series ended, DC collected all four issues in a single volume and sold it through comic shops and through bookstores, which brought the story to a much larger audience and helped DC in its mission to show the world that comics weren't just for kids anymore.

It may be weird to think that in a project where Frank Miller was telling a story about Batman's possible future that he would add something to his history, but Miller managed to pull this off. One minor element was revealing that the movie Bruce and his parents saw the night of their murder was *The Mark of Zorro*, starring Tyrone Power. While it was never expressly stated in the text, this could have been seen as one of the inspirations for Bruce to put on a mask and fight injustice.

The second and more far-reaching addition was a small flashback where we see the Waynes enjoying a picnic on the manor grounds. As Bruce chases a rabbit his father remarks about how fast Bruce can run. Just as he was about to catch the rabbit, Bruce stumbles and falls into a hole in the ground that deposits him in a dark cavern underneath Wayne Manor. Bruce's sudden entry causes the bats that were in the cave to awaken and surround him, with one in particular taking an interest in the boy. The part with the bat flying towards him is played as a dream, but the feeling in the text is that this event actually happened to Bruce. This element would be mentioned later, not only in the comics but in the adapted media, specifically the 1995 film *Batman Forever* and the 2005 film *Batman Begins*.

Miller also recounted the death of the Waynes in the most detailed way possible. The pages where Bruce remembers that night had sixteen, sometimes twenty panels to them with special emphasis on Bruce seeing the gun Joe Chill points at his parents, the shell flying out of the gun after Chill shoots Thomas, the gun getting caught in Martha's necklace, and the necklace breaking with the pearls falling to the ground. This doesn't add any new significant detail to the origin, but it does portray it in the most violent way that had ever been previously shown.

Five months after the final issue of *Batman: The Dark Knight* was released, DC published *Batman* #404. This comic contained the first chapter of a storyline titled "Year One," which would chronicle, as the title suggests, Batman's first year as a crimefighter. *Batman* #404 was written by Frank Miller with art by David Mazzucchelli and the main plot involved Bruce Wayne returning to Gotham City after a number of years abroad, as well as James Gordan moving into town from Chicago to join the Gotham City Police Department. The cover showed a now iconic and oft-repeated visual of young Bruce kneeling in front of the bodies of his parents.

The biggest change that "Year One" made to the origin was having Alfred Pennyworth in Bruce's life much earlier than he had been in the past. Alfred first appeared in *Batman* #16 (April 1943), where he was portrayed as a heavy-set gentleman that shows up on Bruce Wayne and Dick Grayson's doorstep and announces that he is going to be their butler. He was given the surname of Beagle in *Detective Comics* #95 (February 1945) and then in *Batman* #216 (November 1969) his surname is changed to Pennyworth. No matter what his last name was, Alfred was not originally part of Bruce's backstory. He may have been Bruce and Dick's trusted gentlemen's gentlemen, but he came into their lives later in the game. Moving Alfred from that point in Bruce (and Dick's) life to being there from the very beginning gave Bruce a father figure after the death of his parents, albeit one that makes snarky comments about his master's lifestyle choices.

A more minor but still significant addition to the backstory was Bruce's first night out as a vigilante, which was not in costume. Bruce has returned from his travels with all of the tools he needs but something is missing. In March of the *Year One* timeline, he disguises himself as an Army veteran and heads out into the streets of Gotham, which Bruce refers to as "enemy camp." This Gotham is even sleazier and grittier than the city of "There is No Hope in Crime Alley" and is played as an exaggeration of New York City in 1986. The streets of this Gotham are lined with prostitutes and strip clubs and adult movie houses.

The shiny, somewhat happy, version of Gotham from the Fifties and Sixties was gone. Frank Miller took it out back and put two in its head, execution style.

Bruce is propositioned by an underage prostitute, and this puts him into conflict with the girl's pimp Stan. The conflict leads to a full-on brawl with the underaged prostitute, and other sex workers, including a pre-Catwoman Selina Kyle, piling on. The situation deteriorates further when the police arrive, shoot Bruce and take him into custody. Bruce comes to in the back of the police cruiser and despite bleeding from both a bullet and a knife wound Bruce causes the car to crash, saves the cops from a fiery death, and drives home. There, in his father's study, bleeding out and near death he flashes back to the night his parents died. Suddenly a giant bat crashes through the window and lands on a bust in front of Bruce. Then, that edge, that one last piece of the puzzle, the thing that Bruce had been searching for falls into place.

It could be argued that the bat flying through the window and breaking it could have been a hallucination on Bruce's part. Bruce's narration told us that he had seen the bat before, when he was a boy, and it had frightened him. This was more than likely a call back to the first issue of *Batman: The Dark Knight* though there are no allusions to the scene of Bruce falling into the cave.

"Year One" would be the canonical history for Batman for over two decades. Occasionally a new character would be added to the backstory, like Henri Ducard, the man that taught Bruce some of his shadier and brutal lessons, which was revealed in the "Blind Justice" storyline that ran in *Detective Comics* #598 to 600. Then there was Willie Doggett, a bounty hunter that Bruce trained with before he headed back to Gotham, as detailed in *Batman: Legends of the Dark Knight* #1 (November 1989), but the main beats of Miller's version became the gospel other creators would look to when detailing Batman's past.

Another example of this was "The Man Who Falls," an original story written by Denny O'Neil with art by Dick Giordano that first saw print in the *Secret Origins of the World's Greatest Superheroes* trade paperback. This 1990 story solidified Miller's vision by starting with Bruce falling into the cave as a boy and then showing the death of his parents and his aimless early adulthood. O'Neil added that Bruce tried to join the Federal Bureau of Investigation and showed the young man beginning his martial arts training with a sensei named Master Kirigi.

From there O'Neil brought together the threads of the post-*Crisis* origin: Bruce learning from both Ducard and Doggett and commenting on the differences between those men before coming back to "Year One" and Bruce messing up his first night out. "The Man Who Falls" does deviate slightly from what Miller had established. In this telling Bruce was not near death when the bat flew through the window, but the idea remains the same. Miller's version, with a few tweaks here and there from O'Neil, would be the official post-*Crisis on Infinite Earths* history of the Batman.

Post Zero Hour or Joe Chill Has Left the Building

In July of 1994 DC Comics published a five-issue weekly mini-series titled *Zero Hour: Crisis in Time*. This wasn't a sequel to *Crisis on Infinite Earths* so much as an amendment to that event. From 1986 to 1994, DC revamped, rebooted, and/or retrofitted the histories of many of their characters, which made for some dynamic reads, but could play havoc with the continuity of the universe as a whole. A good example of this was a guest appearance by Hawkman and Hawkwoman in *Superman* #18 (June 1988) which later "never happened" when Hawkman received his post-*Crisis* reboot in the pages of the three issue *Hawkworld* mini-series published in 1989.

Batman was more or less exempt from these hiccups thanks in large part to the fact that his post-*Crisis* history was largely free of such problems. The biggest change to his timeline, outside of Alfred being there when he was a child, was that Batman was no longer a founding member of the Justice League of America. The approach the Batman creators took with the character was to focus on his present with the exception of the stories in *Batman: Legends of the Dark Knight*, which told stories of Batman's first year and were, with few exceptions, murky when it came to continuity.

After the fifth issue of *Zero Hour* (which was actually #0 due to the fact that the series started out with #4 and worked its way backwards) most of DC's mainstream line all got their own zero issues. These issues were designed to give the various creators working on their books a chance to either bring the potential new readers that came in with *Zero Hour* up to speed on who their main character or characters were or to reveal any changes made to the backstory of the character or characters. Not counting the Batman family books, like *Catwoman* and *Robin*, Batman received four zero issues for his four titles, *Detective Comics*, *Batman*, *Batman: Legends of the Dark Knight*, and *Batman: Shadow of the Bat* (a series that premiered in 1992), and three of those titles dealt with the newish history of the Batman.

"Creature of the Night" appeared in *Batman* #0 and was written by Doug Moench with art by Mike Manley. During the course of the story, Moench kept a young Bruce Wayne falling into the future location of the Batcave, but added Bruce being told by his mother that the most important thing in life isn't what you own, but who you are as a person. The scene also revealed that Martha did a lot of charity work and that Bruce's father was a doctor even if he really didn't need to work thanks to the Wayne fortune. It's a short scene and doesn't even take up an entire page but it showed more about the Waynes as people than nearly any other origin retelling and explained why Bruce would involve himself in philanthropic work when he wasn't running around the city fighting crime dressed as a bat.

That issue also revealed that the identity of the Waynes' killer was never found. This was a major shift in the background of the character and once again changed Bruce's motivations for becoming Batman. Moench wrote, "Two words boiled from the blackness of his mind: never again. The killer would become a symbol of the faceless crime lurking in every shadow, striking without warning, snuffing lives previous only to those whose futures are shattered by the loss." Removing Joe Chill from the backstory means that this version of Batman was motivated by making sure that what happened to him would never happen to anyone else, ever. It is never made clear in the text why Bruce knowing who killed his parents would make him less likely to become Batman. It's simply stated that Bruce took the pieces of his life that were shattered by this unknown gunman and forged them to help others.

Leslie Thompkins was shown during the funeral flashback and from there we learn that Bruce was not taken in by his Uncle Phillip. Instead, Bruce filed various forms and paperwork that caused him to get "lost" in the system. Instead of going into foster care he remained at Wayne Manor where he trained his body and his mind. The artwork of the next flashback shows us that Bruce still trained with both Master Kirigi and Willie Doggett, so those elements remained in the history.

Batman: Shadow of the Bat #0 had no title for its story, which was written by Alan Grant and art by Bret Blevins. The flashbacks in this issue did not add much to the new history, but it did have a scene showing Alfred and Leslie Thompkins discussing the fact that Bruce doesn't have normal hobbies and spent all of his time either in the gym or reading. This suggested that Leslie was still a part of Bruce's life past the funeral scene that was shown in *Batman* #0.

Detective Comics #0, written by Chuck Dixon with art by Graham Nolan, focused more on how the adult Bruce Wayne created the identity of Batman. There is a scene that showed Bruce discussing the idea of using a bat as the hook for his crime fighting persona. This led into a scene that revealed that Bruce scrapped the idea of his company creating an urban assault cruiser, only to take that design, and other military projects that Bruce cancels, and use them to create the Batmobile and his other equipment. The final flashback that dealt with Bruce's creation of the Batman identity showed him and Alfred spelunking into what would become the Batcave, taking the equipment that Bruce had had Lucius Fox stash in a warehouse, and building the first version of the Batmobile. This issue didn't skimp on the emotional side of Bruce's history, but it did focus more on the nuts and bolts of him building the Batman persona.

These three books, along with *Batman: Year One* and "The Man Who Falls," served as the official, no doubt about it, now and forever history of the Batman for the rest of the Nineties and into the 2000s. Much like the stories in the 1940s, the origin would also rarely be brought up as the Batman titles settled into a pattern of telling their own stories and then joining together into a crossover and then going back to their own stories. It wouldn't be until 2006 that Batman's backstory was once again changed "for good".

Post Infinite Crisis and The New 52 or Joe Chill is Back

At the risk of sounding repetitive, in October of 2005 DC began publishing a seven-issue event titled *Infinite Crisis*. This was a true sequel to the original *Crisis on Infinite Earths*, but in all honesty, the plot of the story didn't matter to Batman's backstory. The only thing that mattered from *Infinite Crisis*, as far as Batman was concerned, is that in the collapsing of realities and the emergence of a new timeline Joe Chill was once again the killer of the Waynes. This isn't even revealed in a dramatic fashion. It was a throwaway line from the ultimate villain of the event. It isn't brought up in the Batman stories that followed either. It was just...there.

Not that it mattered because five years later DC once again went back to the reset well and brought up a bucket containing a heaping, helping dose of something called The New 52. This initiative canceled every mainstream superhero book DC published and replaced them with new series complete with fancy issue #1s. Once again characters like Superman and Wonder Woman were revamped from top to bottom. Batman wasn't.

This made sense considering that in 2011 the Batman titles were among DC's better selling titles. While there were some bigger changes with the extended Bat Family the main Batman titles didn't feel like the continuity had been reset. Again.

At least, that's how it felt at first.

In September of 2012, DC celebrated the first birthday of The New 52 by going back to the creative well of 1994 and having all of their titles come out with a zero issue.

(If at this point in that essay you're thinking that DC seems to do a lot of this whole "rebooting and bringing back things that worked in the past," don't worry because you are absolutely right. They do this. A lot. As of this writing they're still doing it. So, it's not your imagination. It's a thing.)

The New 52 zero issues, much like their 1994 predecessors, were intended to flesh out the history of The New 52 version of the character or team that was the star of the book. This made sense considering that most of the titles that were part of the initial launch of The New 52 took place in the present, five years after the superheroes began to emerge in the new continuity. Having a zero issue gave the creative teams a chance to show some of that history without interrupting the stories they were already telling.

Not counting his supporting heroes, Batman had four ongoing titles at the start of The New 52 with a fifth coming out in July of 2012. Those titles were *Detective Comics*, *Batman*, *Batman and Robin*, *Batman: The Dark Knight*, and *Batman International*. *Batman and Robin* #0 didn't touch on Bruce's backstory in any meaningful way. *Batman Incorporated* #0, which featured a story by Chris Burnham and Grant Morrison with art by Frazer Irving, touched on the *Batman: Year One* version of the origin by showing an injured Bruce watching a bat fly through the window before he reached for the bell to call Alfred for medical assistance. This is important, because it somewhat contradicted a future story that would have its roots in one of the other zero issues published.

Detective Comics (Vol. 2) #0 featured a story titled "The Final Lesson." It took place ten years in the past and showed Bruce Wayne traveling to the Himalayas to learn martial arts from a master named Shihan Matsuda. Bruce does receive that training. Eventually. Like Kirigi before him, Matsuda tells Bruce that he requires several decades to fully train the man. Unlike Kirigi, Matsuda believes that Bruce didn't need to form attachments so that he can better serve the people he wants to protect. Things end badly when Matsuda's wife hires a woman that Bruce had begun a relationship with to kill her husband and Bruce, but Bruce stops the would-be assassin and Matsuda manages to kill his wife, leaving Bruce with his final lesson.... any personal attachments will end badly and in blood.

Batman: The Dark Knight #0 tackled a different aspect of The New 52: Batman's past. Written by Gregg Hurwitz with art by Mico Suayan, this story focused on Bruce just after the death of his parents and his search to find out who killed them and why. This is an obsession that he carries through his childhood and past his graduation from an elite academy. He finally tracks down the man that killed Thomas and Martha and once again it is Joe Chill. Chill's motivations for the crime are very different from the original telling. Instead of being hired by Lew Moxon the robbery was spontaneous and only because Joe wanted Martha's necklace to pay for another bottle of alcohol. Bruce cannot believe it at first, but his parents' murders were not part of some grand conspiracy. They died because an addict needed his fix and he only shot Martha because she screamed and it frightened Chill.

This idea was the best of both worlds of the pre- and post-*Zero Hour* version of the origin. Joe Chill got to stay the murderer of the Waynes, but the killing was still a random mugging gone wrong. The killer had a face and a name, but the reason for their deaths was something as simple as Chill wanting another fix. Bruce had some closure, but it's not the closure he was looking for. He needed their deaths to mean something, to be part of some grand design and the realization that it wasn't drove him to leave Gotham to find some meaning in his life, which eventually leads to the *Detective Comics* story.

Batman (Vol. 2) #0 was the most important in this round of zero issues. "Bright New Yesterday" was written by Scott Snyder with art by Greg Capullo. Of all the creative teams that worked on the various Batman titles at the start of The New 52, Snyder and Capullo were not only the most popular creative team among readers, but they also had the clearest direction for the character. *Batman* Volume 2 was where the big Bat stories took place. The title's zero issue was no exception.

In "Bright New Yesterday," Bruce is undercover with the Red Hood Gang. This is part of his journey to work out exactly how he is going to accomplish his mission. Things don't go according to plan and Bruce barely escapes being killed., Alfred and Bruce are shown to be living in the city and that Alfred wants to go back to Wayne Manor. Bruce pushes back against this and here is where this origin starts to diverge from the previous tellings. Bruce does not think that being Bruce Wayne is important anymore and insists that the idea of Bruce Wayne is just a mask and nothing more. Alfred gives his own push-back, adding that if Bruce doesn't have some kind of social profile the authorities may suspect that he is the one waging war with the Red Hood Gang. At the end of the issue there is a notice that the story will be continued in *Batman: Zero Year*.

Zero Year would turn out to be the new, definitive origin of Batman. This was a bold step. The Miller origin was rock solid. There was no real need for DC to change it, especially since Batman had started down a long road to replacing Superman as DC's flagship character. The first shots across the bow happened in 1989 when the big budget *Batman* film was released into theaters. While there were a few missteps along the way Batman's star began to rise with a popular animated series and three more live action films. It flew into the heavens in 2005 with the release of *Batman Begins*, which led to two sequels that took in over a billion dollars each. Add to that the successful *Arkham* video game franchise and you have a Batman that was omnipresent in the pop culture landscape at a time when superhero films were in the process of becoming more mainstream.

And yet, DC, through Snyder and Capullo, went ahead with changing the origin, but doing so by taking the best elements of what had come before and creating something new.

Batman: Zero Year ran in *Batman* (Vol. 2) #21 to #27, and #29 to #33 and was broken up into three chapters titled "Secret City," "Dark City," and "Savage City." At the start of "Secret City," Bruce is still working on taking down the Red Hood Gang and living in a glorified safe house in the city instead of Wayne Manor. He also wants to continue letting the people of Gotham think that Bruce Wayne is dead. This is an idea that was played with in *Batman Begins*. In that film, Bruce leaves Gotham in his early twenties and is away so long that Alfred has him declared dead. The other New 52 zero issues took cues from *Batman Begins* but *Zero Year* was more overt about it.

Not that the films were the only influences that Snyder drew from. The idea of Bruce leaving Gotham and learning the skills he needed for his mission felt very much like it came from "The Man Who Falls," and Bruce using a disguise to infiltrate the Red Hood Gang as he worked his way to becoming Batman had echoes of Bruce dressing a veteran and taking on a pimp and the police.

Snyder also brought back Uncle Phillip, albeit in a very altered form. In *Zero Year*, Phillip was the one that pushed Bruce to "come back from the dead," though Phillip was a far more nuanced character than the previous version. Not much was done with Uncle

Phillip in the Silver and Bronze Ages. *Zero Year* Uncle Phillip wants Bruce to take over the family business, but Phillip's strategist, Edward Nigma, has his own desire to eliminate Bruce to avoid a protracted power struggle. Phillip does not agree, so Edward hires the Red Hood Gang to kill Bruce. They nearly succeed but a broken and bloody Bruce makes his way to Wayne Manor, , but once there Snyder does his own take on the bat flying in through the window.

Earlier in the story, there is a flashback showing Bruce's father giving him an orb that allows him to see a three-dimensional map of a building. Back in "the present" Bruce finds the orb and drops it into the caves below the Manor and finds himself surrounded by holographic images of the bats that live there. Visually it was a callback to Bruce being surrounded by bats in the cave in *Batman Begins*, but Snyder altered it slightly to allow the event to take place in Wayne Manor. The alchemical combination of the previous origins and the films resulted in an origin that stood on its own and allowed for the comic book version of Batman to step out of the shadow that Frank Miller cast on the character, and it would remain the origin for several years.

In The End…

As of this writing in 2022 the Frank Miller version has returned as the accepted comic book origin of Batman. This more than likely has to do with the various shake-ups DC has gone through since 2016, when The New 52 ended and a new initiative called Rebirth began. Rebirth came and went in two years and there have been several high-profile revamps and initiatives since then and there will more than likely be more of the same down the road as future generations of fans transition from being readers to serving as the storytellers of these characters.

The thing is none of that really matters. DC can reboot and revamp their universe time and again, but Batman's origin will always be some variation of the original version from 1939.

We need to look at Batman's origin as if it were a house. A house built with the finest of wood and concrete with a rock-solid foundation. Over the decades new writers came in and built additions to that house and/or made their own particular renovations. A coat of paint. A new deck. Some of these changes gave the house more value and others were more cosmetic in nature. As time went on a new generation of writers came in and tore down those additions and built new ones, but through it all the house stands strong because its original construction was made of nearly indestructible materials.

Despite Martha's death going through some revisions and reversions, no one has changed the idea that a family of three walked into an alley and only one of them, the son, walked out. That son trained himself and waged a war on crime. Everything else is window dressing. That central idea is so relatable that there hasn't been a need to change it. From children, who are afraid of their parents being taken away from them to adults who feel for the boy that lost those parents, the origin appeals to everyone.

It has been said that Batman is popular because he is so relatable. Anyone can be Batman because he's human and there is something to that, but it misses the overall point. It's not Batman being human that people relate to. It's that he used his trauma to do something positive and make sure that no one else goes through what he did. Most people can't relate to being a billionaire or a master of every known fighting form or the world's greatest detective, but they can relate to wanting revenge on those that hurt them and their family and to ensuring that it never happens again.

It's a simple origin, but still a complicated one. As long as future creators don't mess with that, Batman's place in myth and pop culture is assured.

Michael Bailey started reviewing comics and contributing articles to *The Superman Homepage* in 2001 and has been with that site ever since. He has also written reviews for *Silver Bullet Comics* and *The Spider-Man Crawlspace* and has had work published in Back Issue magazine and in *Ooof! Boff! Splatt! The Subterranean Blue Grotto Essays on Batman '66 - Season Three*. Michael started podcasting in 2007 with the show *Views From the Longbox*. In 2017 he decided to have a single, one-stop home base for the shows he hosts or co-hosts (which include *From Crisis to Crisis: A Superman Podcast*, *The Overlooked Dark Knight*, *The Superman and Lois Tapes*, and *Bailey's Batman Podcast*) and thus was born The *Fortress of Baileytude Podcasting Network*.

CAPTAIN AMERICA

First Appearance: *Captain America Comics* #1, December 20th 1940

Star-Spangled Perspective

By Dan Wickline

In 1940, the comic book world was going through some major changes. DC Comics (then known as National Publications) had struck gold with both Superman and Batman, and their rival, Timely Comics, was trying to keep up. Timely had already launched a book in 1939 called *Marvel Comics* #1 that featured their first superheroes, Namor the Sub-Mariner created by Bill Everett, the Angel by Paul Gustavson, and the Human Torch by Carl Burgos. Most comics of that era would feature one or two stories from the headliner and then be filled with additional tales in various genres. The aforementioned *Marvel Comics* #1 also included a western starting the Masked Raider, a jungle feature with Ka-Zar the Great, another jungle story with Ken Masters and Professor John Roberts, a two-page prose story about auto racing, and five single-panel gag cartoons by Fred Schwab. Publisher Martin Goodman wanted still another character, one that could headline and carry their own title without other characters. He turned to twenty-four-year-old Joe Simon who made a sketch of a patriotic looking character that he originally called "Super American." He would later change it to "Captain America" after realizing there were "too many supers" in comics and then created a young sidekick named Bucky after a friend Simon knew in high school. Goodman liked the concept and to the shock of many, ordered a full issue of adventures to be done right away.

With so many pages to do in such a short time, Simon worried that it would be too much for he and his usual collaborator, twenty-two-year-old artist Jack Kirby, to complete on time and thought about bringing in a couple of additional artists to help. But Kirby, who almost seemed offended by the idea he couldn't do it, convinced Simon that they would be able to handle the project without assistance. The two created seven stories total for the first issue with Simon doing a lot of the layouts, Kirby drawing the characters, and Al Lieberman inking the first story while Simon and Kirby took turns inking the rest. In that first issue, *Captain America Comics* #1, they would give us the straightforward origin of the hero, introduce his sidekick, and the villain who would become his arch-nemesis, all while sending a less-than-subtle message of patriotism to the country.

The character that appeared in that first installment was a very simple hero for a very complicated time. War in Europe had begun, and Adolf Hitler was seen as an evil and dangerous man by some, but not all of the United States agreed with that. There were even groups in America that supported the Nazi Party. There was a wave of isolationism that wanted America to stay out of the brewing war. Between the Great Depression and the tragic losses during World War I, public opinion had moved to non-involvement in European and Asian conflicts and non-entanglement in international politics. There was a belief that any push for intervention overseas were being driven by bankers and arms manufacturers who were only interested in their own profits. The closest thing to a reaction during that time was when President Herbert Hoover established the Stimson Doctrine after Japan invaded Manchuria and was pushing into Northeastern China. The doctrine basically stated that the United States would not recognize territories gained by aggression and in violation of international agreements. This allowed the U.S. to express concern over Japan's actions without committing to any direct interaction. This hands-off approach became an even greater concern when the outbreak of war in Europe in 1939 did nothing to reverse the popular desire to avoid international conflicts. Limited U.S. aid through arms sales to the Allies was seen as acceptable, though, as long as no American lives were put into harm's way.

Isolationism wouldn't work for Simon and Kirby. Both men were children of Jewish immigrants; they understood the horrors of the growing Third Reich and they brought that knowledge to the newsstands. *Captain America Comics* #1 was released on December 20th, 1940, and featured the star-spangled hero on the front cover punching Adolf Hitler in the face. This was anti-isolationism at its finest. There was absolutely nothing subtle about their approach and when you look more closely at the cover, you see other evidence of the message they were sending. Papers on the desk that say, "sabotage plans for USA" and a map of the United States. On the monitor is a man blowing up a U.S. Munitions Works. The imagery let the reader know right away that America wouldn't be safe by choosing to stay on the sidelines.

The stories inside the book weren't about our patriotic hero going to Europe to fight the Germans. They were about the things that Nazis could do here in the States to cause problems, including sabotaging military buildings and killing high ranking officials. These were stories about how the Nazis could already have infiltrated our country and how easily they could cause damage to our democracy. They made the message abundantly clear; Nazis are bad, and we must stop them. Not because Europe needed our help, but because of what they could do to the U.S.A. The country's isolationist attitude could be used as a weapon. The creators were trying to open the country's eyes to the looming threat and with over a million sales of that first issue and many subsequent issues, the message was getting out there.

The first version of the origin story for Captain America was only eight pages and spent surprisingly little time establishing Steve Rogers as a character. We don't even learn his name until the bottom of the seventh page. The story starts with captions telling the reader how the ruthless warmongers of Europe are turning their eyes to a peace-loving America, and how the youth of the country are heeding the call to arms for defense. Then it cuts to a panel where two foreign agents are talking about how easily they joined the army with forged papers, and now they could carry out the Fuehrer's plans. We see them standing outside of American Munitions Inc, a standard-looking factory with the name written on the side, and the caption tells of how much greater the threat of invaders from within by a dreaded fifth column is over the danger of foreign attacks. The first page is split with an obligatory pin-up of a stoic Captain America holding his original shield with an excited Bucky standing a few feet behind. The next page shows the destruction of the munitions factory, and the caption talks about a wave of sabotage crippling the nation's defense industry. We then cut to the White House as two high-ranking Army officials report to President Roosevelt about how their ranks are filled with spies. The president jokes about recruiting a comic book character into the army like the Human Torch (also on sale from Timely), then brings in the head of the FBI, J. Arthur Grover, who is obviously a stand-in for J. Edgar Hoover, who says he has a plan.

As a side note here, even though the art is Jack Kirby, this isn't the art we come to expect from him later when he's co-creating books like the Fantastic Four, the Uncanny X-Men, the Avengers and his eventual return to Captain America. Missing are the big, bombastic poses and art that became his trademark. The panels here, laid out by Joe Simon, feel claustrophobic as if they wanted the reader to feel uneasy. Characters barely fit into panels, or we just see hands or the sides of heads. In one panel two characters have a dialogue box over their heads so we just see their coats. This trapped feeling changes once our hero is revealed and isn't used again in the rest of the book, so it feels like it was a conscious decision to set a dangerous mood for the story.

Those Army officials are asked to disguise themselves in civilian clothing and are taken to a curio shop in the city where an old woman greets them by pulling a gun out of a drawer. When she recognizes Grover, she lowers the gun and tells him that the formula has been found. She leads them through a secret door into a laboratory where the old woman then removes her mask to reveal that she is agent X-13, a beautiful spy for the FBI. This becomes a perhaps-precursor for a much later character and Captain America love interest, Sharon Carter, who is also known as Agent 13. Grover and the Army officials sit down to watch as Professor Reinstein injects a nameless, frail young man with a strange, seething liquid. Reinstein explains to the audience how his formula is enhancing the young man's body and brain tissue until his stature and intelligence is increased to an amazing degree. You have to appreciate the lack of specifics. The professor dubs him Captain America and says that like the captain, America will gain the strength and will to safeguard its shores, once again nailing home that message of anti-isolationism in case anyone had missed it earlier. It's also not too surprising that the origin takes a small, frail guy and turns him into a fighting machine. Neither Simon nor Kirby were large men, and they didn't like bullies, whether from the street corner or another continent. They chose to show the readers that anyone, regardless of their current strength or intelligence, could become a hero and could take on the bullies. This is a trope that gets used many times in comics, from Captain Marvel to Spider-Man.

Then, one of those Army officials turns out to be on "the payroll of Hitler's gestapo" and he pulls a gun, yells "death to the dogs of democracy," and shoots Reinstein, the vial of serum, and finally Grover. The newly minted Captain America leaps forward and starts pounding on the spy before tossing him into some lab equipment where the man is electrocuted, to which the captain says, "Nothing left of him but charred ashes... a fate he well deserved." This shows that early on, the character really didn't have a high regard for life, something we see continue throughout his early adventures as most of his foes end up dead. They didn't make him out to be a murderer or a Punisher-like vigilante, but Cap had no problem using lethal force against an enemy, nor did he feel bad for any of those that died while he was protecting America.

The story then jumps ahead as we get two panels highlighting Captain America now out there stopping spies and making newspaper headlines. But the key is he still hasn't gone overseas; this is all still happening in-country. Then we finally learn that his real name is Steve Rogers and that he's a private in the army assigned to Camp Lehigh. This is where he meets the camp's teenage mascot Bucky

Barnes. It seems kind of odd, but the creators make it seem like every Army base has a teenage mascot. Bucky is a big fan of Captain America and likes to read from the papers to Steve about the hero's exploits. But that very night, Bucky just happens to walk in on Steve changing into his patriotic union suit and realizes that Private Rogers is Captain America. Steve says he should spank the kid, but instead chooses to take the young boy on as his partner, giving him the codename of Bucky. Now, the fact that these stories took place in the U.S. and not in the middle of a warzone makes him having a teenage sidekick a tiny bit less problematic, but not much. It's just another occurrence of that old comic book trope of putting a kid into harm's way to help sales.

The final panel of the origin story is actually an ad for Captain America's official fan club, the Sentinels of Liberty. With a membership, you could join Cap in his war against the spies and enemies in our midst who threaten our very independence. And for a single dime, you could get a real official badge and membership card. The rest of the first issue continued the same types of stories showing enemy agents infiltrating the American way of life and a lot of generals and colonels getting killed. The other big story from the issue is called "Riddle of the Red Skull" and takes up a whopping fourteen pages. This, of course, introduced the villain who would become Captain America's arch-nemesis, except here the Red Skull is actually George Maxon of Maxon Aircraft who uses a crimson skull mask to strike fear into his targets before he poisons them. All of his machinations are orders from Hitler himself who promises the aviation tycoon a big reward when Germany takes over the U.S. Even with the introduction of what would become a classic villain, the story still focuses on the evils of the Nazis and how the U.S. needs to get involved for its own sake.

Captain America Comics would continue on, adding a young writer named Stan Lee to the fold with the third issue to write a short prose story. The only negative thing coming from the debut of the new character was in the form of a potential lawsuit. Another publisher, MLJ Productions, had their own patriotic character called the Shield and while his costume was very different from Captain America's, the design of the Shield's chest looked exactly like Cap's shield. Timely was asked to alter the badge-like design and Goodman agreed. Simon and Kirby changed from the more medieval design to the circular/discus shape that he is known for now. This was a fortuitous change as the circular shield had more uses in the visual medium, allowing the hero to throw it at enemies and bounce it off walls and objects.

Another big change took place around the tenth issue of the title when Simon and Kirby had a falling out with Timely and they left the book and the company. This took place prior to the bombing of Pearl Harbor, meaning at no point were the character's original creators working on the title when America was actually involved in World War II. From that point forward, the title was being handled by Stan Lee and the art team of Al Avison and Syd Shores. And with the United States' entry into World War II, the patriotic feelings in the country helped boost sales of the book. Timely also escalated the propaganda aspects of the stories to match the attitude of the country. And while the character was very popular, the Cap from this era was also quite brutal, killing his foes in various ways including with guns, bombs, and of course his shield. The early message to get people's attention about the horrors of the Nazi movement was no longer necessary. Now the stories were just about beating the enemy.

By September of 1945, the war was coming to an end and America's attention was turning back to the day-to-day world. Cap's popularity and sales took a hit. Lee and company tried to turn him into a more standard superhero. He left the Army and became a teacher, but the audience didn't come along with them. Sales began to plummet, and the company started chasing trends. When romance comics became popular, Bucky was written out and a female love interest named Golden Girl was introduced. As science fiction and horror books became the rage, Cap would take a backseat in his own title as other genres took over. By 1949 the book was renamed *Captain America's Weird Tales* with him becoming nothing more than a narrator before the book was finally canceled altogether with issue #75.

It wouldn't be long before Captain America would rise again, though. Goodman, like Lee, was known for chasing trends and in 1953, the publisher was now calling itself Atlas Comics, and decided to try again with his three bestselling heroes: Namor, Human Torch, and Captain America. This time the captain would be fighting a new enemy, the communists. And whereas after the war, his character had become a teacher, now he was a college professor and Bucky was one of his students. Back were the stories of finding spies within our midst and bringing down saboteurs by any means necessary. In truth the stories read almost the same as the World War II tales, only the political philosophy of the bad guys had changed. The problem was the audience had very much changed and where they had been selling millions of copies in the '40s, Commie-Smasher Cap couldn't make a dent in the market and was canceled after just three issues. While this was an utter failure, this experiment would turn out to be vital to the future of the character when Stan Lee took another crack at the flag-wearing hero a decade later.

In 1962, Goodman learned that his competitors over at DC Comics were having a resurgence with superheroes and even more luck with their Justice League of America property. Goodman turned to Lee and told him to make a new title about a team of heroes. The company was publishing mostly monster books, romance, and westerns at the time and once again changed its name, this time to Marvel Comics. Lee had been thinking of quitting, but his wife urged him to do the book in the way he wanted to, according to Stan, that is. He teamed up with Jack Kirby, who was no longer partnered with Simon, but was back with the company. They came up with a science fiction/monster story where a pseudo family of four ends up with superpowers and stops a subterranean villain and army of monsters. The Fantastic Four was a hit and led to the birth of a new universe of heroic characters. While most of them were original concepts, some of them were variations on the Timely heroes of the '40s. The Human Torch was now a teenage member of the FF and he helped find an amnesiac Prince Namor living on Skid

Row. The Angel was reimagined as a winged mutant and part of the Uncanny X-Men. Even characters like Ka-Zar and the Vision would find their way back into this new age of characters, albeit in different forms.

One of the more popular books, *Avengers*, was actually created because the artist on another title couldn't make his deadline. Bill Everett, creator of Namor, teamed with Stan on a new title called *Daredevil*. But Bill had a problem getting work done on time and the first issue wasn't going to be ready. Because of their distribution deal at the time, with National Publications, aka DC Comics, if Marvel didn't have a book to put out one month, they would lose that spot going forward. So, Stan and Jack threw together a comic using existing characters Iron Man, Thor, Hulk, Ant-Man, and the Wasp and put them up against Thor's brother Loki. The Avengers were an instant hit, but it also became a complication as Stan now had to keep track of what each character was doing in their own title and with the group book. The idea to replace the original lineup started with the decision to bring back Captain America, and while the other heroes were new versions of the older characters, Cap would be the original from the war, just like Namor.

Stan had learned from the failed 1950s revival of the character that he couldn't just be a gung-ho soldier knocking heads and saluting the flag. The world had changed quite a bit in the decade since, and a new, modern Captain America was needed. In a way, this became a new origin story for the hero. His return starts with Namor, seeing a group of men worshiping a figure in a block of ice. Angered by—well just about anything angered Namor, so who knows?—something, Namor threatens the men and tosses their idol into the ocean. The water starts to eat away the ice surrounding it, but the body inside the ice remains in a state of suspended animation until the Avengers happen by in their undersea craft. They pull the body in and recognize his costume as that of the World War II hero Captain America. He, of course, awakens and is unsure of his surroundings, but it is a '60s era Marvel comic, so he fights the Avengers for a few panels before they clear up the misunderstanding and we find out what happened to him in the halcyon days of World War II.

Cap and Bucky were trying to stop a drone plane full of explosives from taking off. They zoomed in on a motorcycle and leapt onto the plane. Bucky was closer and was able to get a solid grip, but Cap couldn't hold on and plummeted into the frozen waters below. He yelled for Bucky to let go, but the teenager reached the cockpit only to discover it was boobytrapped and the plane exploded. Cap would succumb to the freezing temperatures and be encased in ice for over two decades before the Avengers found him. The way Lee and Kirby crafted this story, they did a lot of unique things. They weren't specific about when during the war this event took place, but it was in the European Theater of Operations, meaning it was after the war had begun. And since the *Avengers* issue came out at the end of 1963, it meant that he went into the water at the latest in 1943 if not earlier. This negated the adventures of the character from that date forward, including the 1953 revival. But instead of just pretending those stories never happened, Marvel would later find interesting ways to explain those stories with other men taking on the mantle of Captain America.

This character was very different from the earlier incarnation. He was riddled with guilt over the death of Bucky, something that would reshape the character for decades. He was also a man out of time. Not as drastically as portrayed in the Marvel Cinematic Universe where he was frozen for almost seventy years, the newly thawed hero in the comics had only been on ice for twenty years and while the changes weren't quite as dramatic, they were still a lot to get used to for him. America itself was very different. The Soviets had beaten us into space, the first soldier had died in Vietnam, and we'd just lived through the Cuban Missile Crisis, which brought the idea of nuclear war right to the front door of America. This was the start of the Civil Rights Movement and while Stan Lee had written the overly patriotic version of Cap in the '40s, the '60s called for a more nuanced character, one that didn't stand for the actions of the country but rather for the hope and possibility that came with being an American. The character needed to be someone who didn't just agree with the government because they were elected, but rather someone who believed in the spirit of the nation and judged right and wrong based on equality. One of the biggest reasons for Marvel's success in the '60s, besides the amazing artists, was that Stan could tap into the changing culture and bring it into the stories in a way that felt natural and not preachy.

With Steve Rogers he had a blank canvas in many respects. As we saw earlier, Simon and Kirby spent very little time on who the character was prior to the experiment. He was a 4-F volunteer, and he became a hero. That was pretty much all they needed for the comics during the war. But in this new era, readers wanted more. Now we learned he was born in Brooklyn, NY during the Great Depression and suffered from multiple health issues as a kid. His father died when Steve was a child and his mother died of pneumonia when he was a teenager. When the war started, his desire to serve his country was so strong that he tried multiple times to enlist only to be turned away over and over again until he caught the eye of Project: Rebirth. That little bit of information gave us a much stronger foundation for the character. He grew up in rough times, dealt with multiple tragedies when young and still had such a strong sense of duty that he was willing to go to war even when he wasn't physically capable of fighting. This established that the hero was the scrawny kid from Brooklyn, not what the super-soldier serum did to him.

This backstory made the character more relatable for readers and that's what the audience was looking for. Spider-Man wasn't popular just because of the cool suit Steve Ditko created; it was also the real-world problems, the death of Uncle Ben, and trying to choose between stopping a bank robbery or getting the medicine to save his aunt. Iron Man was a super-rich playboy inventor, but what humanized him was a chunk of shrapnel that sat mere centimeters from his heart that could kill him at any time, yet he still put on the armor and tried to save the world. The Marvel Age was about heroes with real lives and real problems that readers could identify with. It's why a flag wearing symbol of the country that people were starting to question still not only connected with the audience but found new ways to reach out to them. Lee and Kirby took the problem of how to make a World War II hero fit into a '60s world and made that the very question of the series: Steve Rogers was trying to answer that question too. They put aside the soldier and focused on what made him a good man. Readers were less concerned with his relevance and more concerned with the character dealing with his newfound feelings of isolation and grief.

The character's return was a success, and not only did he become a regular member of the Avengers, eventually becoming the leader and by *Avengers* #16—he would lead a whole new team with Hawkeye, Black Widow, Scarlet Witch and Quicksilver—but he would also become one of the stars of a split book called *Tales of Suspense*. In November of 1964, Captain America and Iron Man shared the spotlight in *Tales of Suspense* #59 with each character getting a ten-page story of their own. Stan and Jack told a story about Cap staying at Avengers Mansion, mainly because he doesn't have anything else in his life except being an Avenger. A group of gangsters decide to attack the mansion as a team using high tech gear only to find and be defeated by the single hero at home. It's pretty much a story to showcase Jack's amazing art. There really isn't a plot, but we do get to see that Cap is being very introspective and he gets upset looking through an old scrapbook of his time in the war. He feels isolated and guilty for what happened to Bucky. Again, this is very different from the Cap who, when in the first Red Skull story back in 1941 he was asked by Bucky why he didn't stop the Skull from rolling over onto the poison syringe, simply replied, "I'm not talking."

Though they'd done a couple of issues with Cap in the modern day, in *Tales of Suspense* #63, they decided to move his stories back to the war era. The idea was to take the original stories from *Captain America Comics* and tell them again, but these remakes were done with a modern (for the time) spin. They started with the origin story. The first big change you notice is the feeling of the layouts. Gone was the claustrophobic feeling that Simon had introduced. Kirby started with a full-page splash of Captain America and Bucky standing on a fallen Nazi flag with explosions going off behind them. The heroes are in action poses taking up the majority of the page rather than being jammed together into half the page, pushed into the spine of the book. Everything on the page is about excitement and highlighting the characters. The story can wait a page. In big letters it says "The Origin of Captain America" rather than the simple "Meet Captain America" that had been tucked up in the top right corner in the original issue.

Gone are the jingoistic captions and talk about the Fifth Column having infiltrated the ranks of the Army. Adding a touch of humor, one of the men being tested for the draft tries to get out of it by claiming hay fever only to have the doctor assure him that the army will give him tissues and then approves the man for service. There's still the sabotage of a munitions plant, but we learn of what it was through dialogue, not having the description written on the building itself. The Army officials visiting President Roosevelt aren't there because they're concerned about foreign spies in their midst, but rather they're giving a report on "one of the strangest experiments of all, Operation Rebirth." The anti-isolationist message is completely gone, which makes sense as the country wasn't on the precipice of a world war in 1965. But Stan still wrote in his hyperbolic style and spoke of America flexing her mighty armed muscles and her growing arsenal of freedom.

The generals learn that the serum is ready and are led to the curio shop by two intelligence agents. They are again met by an elderly woman with a gun. She's identified as Agent R and leads the men to the lab where, as before, she removes her disguise to reveal the face of a beautiful young woman. Now there is another doctor inside the viewing area who explains that it took them months to find a proper 4-F volunteer whose body would react properly to the tissue building chemical. In the original version, Steve had just volunteered for military service and was rejected earlier that same day. No testing to see if he was a good candidate, they just led him in and stuck a needle in his arm. Now we see Rogers enter with, as Stan says, "obvious nervousness, yet with a firm, fearless tread..." He is described as a thin, almost sickly-looking youth. Then we get the caption that shows the major difference between the comics of the '40s and of the '60s. Whereas who the volunteer was didn't matter before, now we get a caption that tells us all about Steve Rogers: "Too puny, too sickly to be accepted by the army. Chosen from hundreds of similar volunteers because of his courage, his intelligence, and his willingness to risk death for his country if the experiment should fail." That paragraph drives home once again that Steve Rogers was the hero, the super-soldier serum only gave him the tools to make a difference. That seemingly simple change may be the number one reason why Captain America is as popular as he is today while other patriotic-themed heroes fell by the wayside.

Another thing this version of the origin adds is a sense of danger. Reinstein tells Rogers in the first origin, "Don't be afraid, son. You're about to become one of America's saviors." No doubt or hesitation at all. Reinstein knew exactly what was going to happen and that it would work out just fine. Here, Professor Reinstein has become Dr. Erskine, and he's not quite as confident. He first tells Steve to drink quickly before the chemicals lose their potency and wishes him good luck. He then turns to the audience and says, "If we have erred, Rogers will be dead within seconds! For he is drinking the strongest chemical potion ever created by man!" He then goes on to say what'll happen if they succeed, which would be to create an army of super-soldiers with reflexes, physical condition, and courage second to none. Reinstein was focused on making "super-agents" who would be a terror against spies and saboteurs. Also, Reinstein's formula worked on intelligence too, Erskine's not so much. Steve would have to use the smarts that he brought to the table.

The next interesting change from the original comes in some exposition from one of the guests who explains that the operation is such a secret that the formula has never been written down and only Erskine has it committed to memory. None of that came up in the first origin. Trying to duplicate the super-soldier serum has been an often-used plot point for many comics and the creation of other Marvel characters. It's also been a major impetus in the Marvel Cinematic Universe. You can argue that it was implied in the original when Reinstein is killed and then the formula vial is shot by the spy, but this version makes it much cleaner and clearer for the reader. From there things run pretty parallel as a spy pulls a gun and shoots Erskine, leaving the U.S. with just one super-soldier. Steve jumps into action to stop the spy, but this time when the man is running towards the electrical omninverter, Steve tries to warn him. The man, of course, still runs into the coils and gets electrocuted. Not sure how Steve knows the machine is an electrical omninverter, but hey, the important thing is he tried to stop the man from dying, another plus in this new origin's favor. But as Stan says, "Thus, a champion of freedom is born—and a foe of liberty meets his death, in a truly symbolic revelation of things to come!"

The last five pages of the new origin expand on what was covered in two half-pages in the original. We get a full-page of Captain America in action against various non-specific thugs and, like in the original, we see newspapers with headlines touting the heroics of our Star-Spangled Hero. And they keep with the idea that all of this fighting takes place in the U.S. with him protecting defense plants, stopping spies, and bringing in saboteurs. Then another page introduces us to his secret identity as bumbling army private Steve Rogers who is always getting in trouble with his sergeant, all to keep anyone from suspecting who he really is. We are also introduced to Fort Lehigh's camp mascot Bucky Barnes, but now we learn a bit more about the teen as a caption tells us that when Bucky's G.I. father was killed during training, the orphaned boy was adopted by the camp. And while I can't see that happening in real life, at least they tried to explain why a military base would have a teenager running around in a military uniform. We then get an almost identical panel of Steve changing into his costume and Bucky walking in to discover his friend is Captain America. But instead of Cap saying he should "tan his hide" before deciding to take the boy on as a sidekick, Cap blames himself for not being more cautious and it's Bucky who suggests, now that he knows Cap's identity, he has to take him on as a partner. Cap says, "Looks like I've got no choice." Again, this is a very different take on the original scene and while still a hero taking a boy into a war, at least it wasn't his idea to do it.

Cap tells Bucky that he's going to need to be trained and when we do see Bucky in action, it's supposed to be after months of intense training. We see them take on a group of saboteurs coming from a U-boat with a haul of explosives. Cap leaps into the fray, but Bucky holds off and takes on one guy that is trying to shoot Cap from a distance. Even in the fight, Cap is keeping an eye on his sidekick and once they've taken out the thugs, they send the explosives back at the U-boat, blowing it up. It's a short little mission, but enough to establish that there was some training, and it was more than just, "Oh you found out who I am, here's a costume, try to not get killed." Stan was known for not liking sidekicks and you see that they really don't come up much in Marvel comics outside of the characters created in the '40s. Partners were fine and Captain America would end up working with another partner, the Falcon, not long after his return, but teen sidekicks weren't a Marvel thing and really only showed up in stories from the past like the Tales of Suspense run or when Cap and Bucky teamed up with Namor, the Android Human Torch and his sidekick Toro in the pages of the Invaders, stories also set during World War II.

This revised origin kept the heart of the story the same but took the time to establish more about the characters of Steve Rogers, Bucky Barnes, and even Dr. Erskine. It reset the characters to ones that would be interesting to the readers in the '60s, but also give Stan a way to try and connect that audience of the past to a more modern readership. Captain America became a bridge to deal with the highly charged political issues of the day, but through the prism of someone from an older generation, which Stan was part of. In many ways his writing was timeless as he could voice the teenaged Peter Parker, the jet-setting Tony Stark, the man-out-of-time Steve Rogers, the man-monster Ben Grimm, or even the space-faring loner Norrin Radd. Stan was able to find a unique voice and point-of-view for each character he wrote and with this new version of Cap's origin, Stan was able to put the framework in for who Captain America would become. You could argue that the revised origin for Stan and Jack's Captain America ran from frail Steve Rogers entering Dr. Erskine's lab all the way through until he's found in the water by the Avengers, as the death of Bucky is as crucial to making the hero as him being injected with the super-soldier serum.

Two issues later, the duo would retell the hero's first adventure against the Red Skull, and while a lot of the same elements were used, the tone of the story changed quite a bit with the Red Skull not killing his targets but knocking them out to prevent them from discovering the truth. He was a German spy who replaced John Maxon to sabotage the aircraft company. And here the Red Skull escapes rather than dies on his own syringe. The idea that the skull head was just a mask is used here as well, but we know that they would change that in the near future. And by the near future I mean the very next issue where we see an original story that shows Captain America captured by the Red Skull. The Nazi villain then explains how he was personally selected and trained by Adolf Hitler and then given the mask and uniform that he now wore. This would lead into a multi-part story where Red Skull brainwashes Cap and sends him off to assassinate a high-ranking Army official. It's obvious from this early tale that Marvel recognized what a good villain Simon and Kirby had created with the Red Skull, which is ironic as when Simon was thinking up Captain America in the first place, he decided to start with the villain and chose Hitler then created Cap to counter him…only to create Cap's true foil in the very same pages.

With Captain America's origin changing to include going into the ice during the war, there were years of *Captain America Comics* published in the mid to late '40s and the three in the '50s that suddenly fell out of continuity. Writer Roy Thomas and artist Frank Robbins fixed part of that in the pages of *The Invaders*, though. After the real Cap and Bucky disappeared in 1945, President Harry S. Truman recruited another patriotic costumed hero, William Naslund, aka the Spirit of '76, to take up the mantle along with a young man named Fred Davis as Bucky. They teamed with Namor and the Red Guardian to stop the Nazis from destroying the Potsdam Conference. Naslund would serve as Cap for a while before being killed while protecting a young congressional candidate named John F. Kennedy. The shield was then picked up by Jeffrey Mace, who had previously been known as the Patriot. He had no Bucky but was partnered with a woman named Betsy Ross aka Golden Girl who he would end up marrying; he retired as Captain America in 1949. That pretty much covered the original run of *Captain America Comics*.

The Commie-Smasher Captain America was a bit more interesting. This was a college professor named William Burnside who, through research, discovers the Nazi files on Captain America including his true identity and the super-soldier formula. With this knowledge, he approaches the FBI and forces them to agree to use him as the new Captain America during the Korean War. He legally changes his name and has plastic surgery to look like Steve Rogers. He has a student, Jack Monroe, who has a similar obsession with Captain America and when the Red Skull attacks the United Nations, Burnside injects himself and Monroe with the untested formula. While it gives them the strength and reflexes, the formula is missing the vita-ray component and causes psychotic symptoms. The two become unreliable, paranoid, and extremely aggressive. The FBI places them both in suspended animation but they are revived and sent off to kill the real Captain America and his new partner the Falcon. When they fail, Burnside ends up in the hands of Dr. Faustus, who brainwashes him into being the villainous Grand Director and pits him against Rogers. While not part of Faustus' scheme, Monroe would have his own issues for years until eventually being rehabilitated and taking on the mantle of Nomad, a name Steve Rogers used for a short while in the '70s. Needless to say, clever creators like Steve Englehart, Sal Buscema, Roger Stern, and Jim Shooter found unique ways to explain away the drastic changes in Captain America's origin without just negating the appearances. And in the case of Burnside, to explain away the violent nature of the characters' appearances and come up with a new villain to boot.

At this point we have a thoughtful, heroic character who symbolizes the hope of our nation, but who is willing to stand up to the government when it goes against the very ideals the country was founded on. This is the Captain America that we've seen for the last six decades and that continues to be popular with readers. But it wasn't the last time part of his origin was tweaked. The two main components to the character's origins were the Project: Rebirth experiment and the death of Bucky Barnes. That latter part of that would be changed by writer Ed Brubaker along with artists Steve McNiven and Mike Perkins in a new *Captain America* #1 in 2005. It's a story that starts with the murder of Red Skull by a mysterious figure who claims the Cosmic Cube for his boss, General Lukin, while Steve Rogers is having dreams about the past that don't match up to his memories. He sees Bucky dying of a gunshot wound instead of in the exploding plane. Cap is called in by S.H.I.E.L.D. to help investigate the death of the Red Skull and the now missing Cosmic Cube while the mysterious assassin tracks down and kills Jack Monroe, the Bucky from the '50s. Nick Fury sends Cap to Washington to investigate an incident at Arlington National Cemetery where he discovers two headstones desecrated with bullets, those of William Naslund, and Jeffrey Mace, the other two Captain Americas from the '40s. Cap is then attacked by Crossbones, but while fighting he is flooded with inaccurate memories involving Bucky and Baron Zemo. Cap is too distracted to fight, and Crossbones doesn't want to win that way, so he leaves him, but tells Cap that he had been led there by a Russian.

We learn that the whole thing is a plan by Lukin and his Winter Soldier to manipulate Cap's mind. For Lukin it's a matter of revenge, for back when Lukin was a boy, his village was destroyed in a battle between Captain America and the Red Skull. Lukin's plan was to set off a major bomb in Philadelphia and make Cap watch. But Sharon Carter has a chance to see Lukin's assassin and she tells Cap that she believes that it's the real Bucky Barnes. While trying to help survivors, Cap comes face-to-face with the Winter Soldier and asks him if he's Bucky, but the Winter Soldier doesn't know who Bucky is. Falling debris separates the two and the conflict is postponed. Fury then briefs Cap on the Winter Soldier, a Russian assassin operating from 1955 well into the 1970s. Facial recognition scans put the same man at many assassinations through that time, but the person has barely aged, and he looks like an adult Bucky Barnes. Dubbed the Winter Soldier, he would show up on the radar for a few months before disappearing again for years. Fury believed he was the real Bucky.

Steve is left a mysterious file in his apartment with the history of the Winter Soldier. The mystery man was indeed James "Bucky" Barnes and the Soviets had recovered his body from the English Channel. Though he was dead and missing an arm, his body was frozen, and they were able to revive him. He resisted them at first, but intensive brainwashing overwrote who he was, creating a blank slate for them to program. They built a bionic arm for him and trained him to be an assassin. Occasionally while on missions, Bucky would begin to remember his true self and fight against his orders. The Soviets would then go through the brainwashing procedure again. This is why he was returned to stasis regularly— because they couldn't keep him programmed. By the end of the Cold War, he was decommissioned and put into storage where he was basically lost for years. Later he would be discovered and revived by Lukin and used as his greatest weapon.

While there is a lot more to what happened around the two, the conflict between Captain America and the Winter Soldier eventually led to them fighting for the Cosmic Cube with Steve trying desperately to get Bucky to remember who he was. But when the battle turns, and Cap gains the Cube, he uses the power of the object to restore Bucky's memories. Bucky tells Cap he should've just killed him. The character is riddled with guilt for all that he's done as a pawn for the Soviets. And while he destroys the Cosmic Cube and escapes, Cap is certain that his friend is still out there. Oh, and as a side effect of using the Cube, the Red Skull's mind ends up inside of General Lukin. You didn't really think they'd kill off the Red Skull, did you?

This was an incredibly risky change to make to Captain America's origin. There are certain touchstone moments in comics that wholly define a character: the death of Bruce Wayne's parents, the destruction of Krypton, the death of Uncle Ben. These are crucial to the hero's journey and if you take that away, even later in life, there is the possibility of drastically changing a character. At this point though, the guilt over Bucky's death is deeply ingrained in Steve Rogers, making him want to help others and do what he believes is right. And in a way, that guilt shifted from not saving his friend to not believing that his friend was still alive and finding a way to save him decades earlier. It's a little surprising that Brubaker doesn't address the anger Cap would feel towards Fury for not letting him know that they believed Bucky was alive and working for the Soviets.

The death of Dr. Erskine and with it his super-soldier serum has been a catalyst for many things in Marvel Comics and their film franchises. In the MCU, Bruce Banner was unknowingly working to recreate the serum when he became the Hulk. Red Guardian was the Soviets' version of it as was the Winter Soldier program. There are many other ties including a new version of the serum that gets brought up in *The Falcon and the Winter Soldier* TV series, which also introduces us to Isaiah Bradley. Bradley was another man to become Captain America, but not by choice. In the 2002 comic series *Truth: Red, White & Black*, writer Robert Morales and artist Kyle Baker take us back to the war as the U.S. government forcibly recruited three hundred African American soldiers to be test subjects in an experiment to recreate Dr. Erskine's formula. To keep the project secret, the men's families were told that the soldiers all died. This turned out to be prescient as only a handful of the recruits survived the process. The creators basically paralleled the infamous Tuskegee Study of the '30s that gave African Americans syphilis, lied to them about getting the proper medical treatment and then kept track of them over forty years.

In the comic, those that survived the experiments were used as covert soldiers for a while, but members of the unit died off, eventually leaving only Bradley. His next assignment was basically a suicide mission, to go into Germany, find the man behind the Germans' super-soldier program, kill him and destroy a Nazi death camp in Schwarzebitte. Before he left, Bradley stole a Captain America uniform and one of the original badge-shaped shields and used them on his mission. His mission was a success, but he was captured, then rescued by German resistance and fought his way out of the country, returning home months later. Upon his return, he was court-martialed and sent to prison for stealing the Captain America uniform. He spent seventeen years in prison and only the persistence of his wife, who never believed he had died, writing to the president every month finally got him released just as Kennedy was being inaugurated. His grandson, Eli Bradley, would later become a hero called Patriot and join the Young Avengers. Eli wasn't born with powers and for a long time used drugs to gain strength, but after giving it up and trying to be a hero without them, he was wounded and received a blood transfusion from his grandfather, giving him the same powers.

In one of the most controversial storylines over the last decade, Marvel presented a 2017 company-wide crossover story by Nick Spencer and Daniel Acuna called "Secret Empire" that involved a sentient Cosmic Cube named Kobik who was manipulated by the Red Skull to create the ultimate version of Captain America, one that would be loyal to Hydra. Kobik did this by creating an alternate timeline where Steve Rogers first came in contact with Hydra at the age of six. His family was introduced into a Hydra community that killed Steve's abusive father and when his mother, Sarah, tried to escape with him, she was seemingly killed as well. Steve was taken to a Hydra training facility called The Keep where they tried to indoctrinate him but failed, and Steve tried many times to escape. He was finally befriended by Daniel Whitehall, who was also known as The Kraken. He was able to convince Steve to embrace Hydra's ideals and prove himself to the order. Steve worked his way up in the ranks and was eventually assigned to return to the United States and to assassinate Dr. Erskine. He eventually succeeded with the help of his handler, Baron Helmut Zemo, and ended up as a candidate for the continued Project Rebirth now being headed up by Arnim Zola, who was secretly still loyal to Hydra. Steve would become Captain America, but all the while remained a sleeper agent for Hydra. This version of Captain America would eventually become

Captain Hydra and stick around for a few years before the story concluded, the character was killed and the Steve Rogers from the real timeline returned. While this altered version of Captain America's origin pertained only to the Secret Empire/Civil War II storyline, Spencer pretty much "kitchen-sinked" it by putting in as many of Cap's villains as he could fit. What made it even more interesting is that Marvel presented it in the main continuity and readers rebelled against the change. No one truly believed that Captain America was going to be a Hydra agent forever, but it shook up the status quo so much that fans really weren't sure.

Another variation on Cap's origin came in 2002 with the creation of Marvel's Ultimate line of comics. This was a new universe started in the 2000s that tweaked a lot of the characters. Many of these changes ushered in by writers Brian Michael Bendis and Mark Millar, would end up being incorporated into the foundation of the MCU. One of the biggest changes to Ultimate Cap's origin involves Bucky. Here Bucky isn't a camp mascot, but rather Steve's best friend growing up who helped protect the frail boy from bullies. This change removes the awkward idea that Captain America would train and take a teenage boy into battle, something that definitely wasn't going to fly in the 21st century. This change was used in *Captain America: The First Avenger* feature film and his friendship with Bucky was the impetus for him disobeying orders and going off to rescue Barnes and his unit after they were captured by the Germans. The big difference between the two versions is that after Erskine is killed, MCU Cap is turned into a propaganda tool to help sell war bonds, while Ultimate Cap meets with President Roosevelt who encourages him to commit to the American war effort. Another change is in the Ultimate universe, Bucky becomes a war photographer and Cap hangs out with "Lucky" James Howlett who would later become Wolverine. In this version of Steve's attempt to stop the missile and end up in the frozen water, Bucky isn't involved so when Cap is thawed in the future, he doesn't have the grief of losing his friend. This plays out with a Cap that is more cynical and violent than the one we see in the main universe or in the films.

While the rest of the MCU is a mix of Ultimate, Main universe and some original material, another thing they borrowed from the Ultimate Universe is changing the uniform to feel more utilitarian and militaristic rather than something with swashbuckler boots and wings on his mask. The films took time to pay homage to the original design by Joe Simon in Steve's time in the USO, but as soon as he heads off to battle, he grabs a real helmet and puts on a web belt and a leather jacket before going off to save Bucky.

There are many examples of character origins being changed over the years by writers putting in hooks for new stories. The addition of a childhood friend who would later become a villain, a college love interest that could come back to be a major plot point, or the introduction of a massive conspiracy involving the hero's parents that they knew nothing about. These are changes for story's sake and oftentimes end up never being used or spoken of again. A long-lost brother gets introduced, used as a pawn against the protagonist and then disappears like *Happy Days'* Chuck Cunningham when a new writer comes on board. These are not the type of changes that have happened to Captain America. The first major changes to the character were done by the original artist and a writer who had been working on the character for two decades. They understood the character as well as anyone and made the changes not for a specific story idea, but to add more depth and find a way to make him relevant. They did this by making small tweaks to the origin, giving the character more compassion and heart. They left him as a product of World War II instead of moving him up to the Korean Conflict or Vietnam. They made him far more introspective and even suffered from post-traumatic stress disorder even though real understanding of the disorder wouldn't come for another decade.

When Captain America was created, it was by two young men in their early 20s worried about the growing threat of Nazi Germany on the countries their parents had immigrated from. At the time neither Joe nor Jack knew anything about war. That would change shortly after. While Joe served, he would never return to write the character. Both Stan and Jack spent time in the war. Stan worked as part of the training film division, making posters, and writing scripts for propaganda films. Jack wasn't so lucky. He was assigned to be a member of the infantry and was part of the second wave of soldiers to hit the beach at Normandy the day after the initial landing. He saw action, facing down the enemy and even taking lives. At one point he told how in one battle only four members of his unit came out alive. That's the other major difference between the Captain America of the early 1940s and the one that the Avengers rescued in the 1960s; one of the creators had gone to war and saw it firsthand. Jack knew what it was like to be talking to someone one second and to have them killed the next. With the way that Marvel did comics in those early days, it's hard to delineate who did what but often times Stan would discuss the plot with the artist, in this case Jack who would then draw the story and bring it back. Oftentimes with notes in the borders to explain what is going on in the story. Stan would then script the dialogue, sometimes taking the notes into consideration, other times going a completely different direction. So, at this point it's impossible to say which of the men pushed for the changes to Steve Rogers or if it was something they came up with together, but the end result is a character who understands the horrors and necessities of war and no longer aggrandizes it. This new version values human life, regardless of which side they're on and stands up for the ideals of the United States rather than just for the men in charge.

None of this depth of character existed in the early adventures and it explains why the hero's popularity plummeted so much when the war was over, and America's patriotic drive was refocused onto other things. Without the clear-cut villainy of the Nazi party, a jingoistic hero no longer had a place in an America that was starting to question authority and the status quo. Stan and Jack gave us a hero rocked by the horrors he had seen, one that was also questioning authority and the status quo, one that was looking for his own place in the changing world. Did they know these changes would connect with readers and bring the once popular hero back to prominence, making him an icon who would not only continue for another sixty-plus years but also turn into a major motion picture franchise? Probably not. It's more likely that they just thought it would make for a good story, and it definitely did.

Dan Wickline is the creator of the Legacy of Lucius Fogg novels as well as having written issues of *ShadowHawk, 30 Days of Night, Grimm Fairy Tales*, and his recent hit series *The Freeze*. In prose he's worked on The Phantom, Green Hornet, and the Avenger short stories as well as full-length novels of Vampirella, Purgatori and an adaptation of *The Boys*. If you're a fan of the television series *Dexter*, you may have seen Dan as comic writer Denny Foster in the second season where he was found dead on a comic shop floor having been killed by a snow globe.

WONDER WOMAN

First Appearance: *All-Star Comics* #8, October 21st 1941

The More Things Change...

By Sam Agro

Way, way back in 1978, the Who released a song in which they posed the deceptively simple question, "*Who are you?*" There are no easy answers to that query, let me tell you. Most of us spend a lifetime trying to understand who we are, what we want, and why we are hanging around on this crazy, spinning space-rock.

What makes a person who they are, and what they are, anyway?

If you are like me, and by that I mean mercilessly introspective, then you spend a great deal of time attempting to divine and define exactly that. Human beings can be a mass of clashing emotions and elusive motivations and the pursuit of Socrates's simple edict "*To know thyself is the beginning of wisdom.*" can prove a daunting enterprise.

One important factor in knowing who we are as individuals is understanding our roots and origins. Family history is certainly part of this, but much more crucial is the interplay of our lives; the events, experiences, and observations that helped fabricate our identity, those formative experiences that saddle us with so many traits and tendencies, both good and bad, for years to come.

The imaginary characters who people fiction can sometimes be as complex and elusive as we denizens of the real world. When we read stories, we search for ourselves in the characters we find there. We seek out the overlap between what *we* are and what *they* are, so that we might empathize with their trials and tribulations, share in their joys and victories, and immerse ourselves in their exploits. In the world of comics, it is the task of writers and artists to do the same. They must uncover their own unique connections to a character and mine those areas of commonality to connect the reader to their fictitious avatars.

The inciting incident that launches a comic book character from the mundane to the exceptional is generally referred to as their *origin story*. The origin story is often boiled down to a single catalytic event: Peter Parker gets chomped on by a radioactive spider and develops arachnid-based abilities, a dying alien gifts fearless Hal Jordan with a special ring of great power, brainy Bruce Banner gets caught in the fallout of a gamma bomb explosion and occasionally transforms into a muscular, green rage monster. There may be tertiary elements exerting some influence, but often it is these shining flashes of impetus that are the key to all that comes after.

The inciting event for Wonder Woman is a little more difficult to pin down than some. One might suggest it's the arrival of Steve Trevor on Paradise Island, another might point to her choice to disobey her mother and compete for the right to go out into man's world— but wait, I'm getting a little ahead of myself.

Our mandate, as contributors to this volume, is to chronicle the myriad evolutions of the origin story of our chosen character over the course of their many decades of publication. Wonder Woman's tale has transformed a fair bit over time, sometimes based on the inspirational impulses of the creative team of the moment, due to outside pressures, or in a conscious effort to adapt to the changing social zeitgeist.

Genesis: All-Star Comics #8 and Sensation Comics #1

Wonder Woman's first appearance in *All-Star Comics* #8 weighs in at a compact nine pages, including some pages of illustrated text. It's really two origin stories, that of Wonder Woman, and also the Amazons of Paradise Island. I'm going to describe this premiere story in explicit detail, since it's the foundation for all the transformations that follow. I view this and *Sensation Comics* #1 together as Wonder Woman's complete origin story because I believe that leaving Paradise Island and establishing her alter ego are legitimate elements of that origin.

The first tale opens on a lovingly rendered action shot of our new heroine, by artist H. G. Peter. Creator Charles Moulton, aka William Moulton Marston, begins the story with a single large paragraph, a bold pronouncement of Wonder Woman's innate superiority to men:

"At last, in a world torn by the hatreds and wars of men, appears a woman to whom the problems and feats of men are mere child's play- a woman whose identity is known to none, but whose sensational feats are outstanding in a fast-moving world! With a hundred times the agility and strength of our best male athletes and strongest wrestlers, she appears as though from nowhere to avenge an injustice or right a wrong! As lovely as Aphrodite, as wise as Athena—with the speed of Mercury and the strength of Hercules—she is known only as Wonder Woman, but who she is, or whence she came, nobody knows."

That is a helluva declaration!

Here Moulton firmly establishes the foundations of Greek mythology he will frequently utilize and sets this opening page proclamation as a standard fixture in successive stories. This bombastic credo also reflects Marston's personal (or at least stated) belief that women were equal to, and perhaps in some ways superior to, the male of the species.

Marston then leaps immediately into the story as two women, one of whom is referred to as "princess," watch an airplane crash near their uncharted island home. (For the bulk of the story, she is addressed only as "princess" by the other Amazons, or as "daughter" by her mother.) The two women are shocked to discover the injured person in the plane is—of all things—a *man*! The princess scoops him up like a baby and runs him to a nearby hospital. Hippolyte, the queen of Paradise Island and mother to the princess, looks over some papers found in the airman's pocket and discovers he is Capt. Steve Trevor, of U. S. Army Intelligence.

She orders Trevor be cared for, and the princess, who appears to be a trained nurse, takes it very seriously. So seriously, in fact, that the tattle-tale doctor reports her overly attentive ministrations to Hippolyte. "*So she is in love!*" declares the queen, adding, "*I was afraid of that!*" and orders the princess banned from the hospital. When the princess complains, Hippolyte relates the origin story of the Amazons, which goes essentially as follows:

In ancient Greece, the mighty Amazons were a big deal, but Hercules decided to prove himself their better. Thanks to a magic girdle gifted to her by Aphrodite, Hippolyte was able to easily defeat the big lug. Falling back on trickery, Herc steals the girdle and enslaves the Amazons, shackling their wrists. Aphrodite lets them suffer for a while, but eventually relents and returns Hippolyte's magic girdle. The Amazons defeat their male oppressors, steal their fleet, and set sail for Paradise Island, where Aphrodite decrees they must remain separate from the world of men. They must also continue to wear their shackles as bracelets to remind them of the indignity of their subjugation.

In their new home, the Amazons live peaceful, idyllic, and eternal lives, as long as they never again allow themselves to again be beguiled by men. Which is why, the queen explains, Steve Trevor must return to his world asap! Isolated on their island the Amazons have developed better weapons and flying machines than the outside world, and they have the Magic Sphere, which gives them an abundance of information on the world, past and present. Hippolyte takes her daughter to see said sphere, (which is confusingly flat) and they gaze back in time at Steve Trevor's recent adventures.

The debut of Wonder Woman coincided with the entry of the United States into WWII, and the magic flashback finds Trevor taking it upon himself to bust up a Nazi spy ring. The results of his bold, one-man efforts are unfortunate. Trevor is defeated, knocked unconscious, and placed on a robot plane which is sent to bomb his own airbase. Trevor regains consciousness and takes control of the robot plane. He gives chase, hoping to bring down the Nazi aircraft, but before he can do so he runs out of fuel and crashes on Paradise Island.

Hippolyte decides to consult Aphrodite and Athena for advice, and they tell her to choose the strongest and wisest Amazon to accompany Trevor back to the good old US of A, which is, after all, *"the last citadel of democracy, and of equal rights for women."* Whew! That assertion didn't age very well, did it?

Hippolyte arranges a tournament to pick the most wondrous of the Amazon women, and immediately forbids her daughter from competing. However, when a single mystery Amazon shows up at the games wearing a domino mask, no one seems the least bit suspicious. After racing against a deer, and many other unnamed tests, the field is winnowed down to two women, the masked Amazon, and one other. To break the tie, they face off in the most dangerous test of all, Bullets and Bracelets! The masked competitor wins the contest and reveals her true identity to Hippolyte as her own daughter. The queen allows that the princess has fairly earned her stripes. Or stars, at least, which adorn the costume designed by Hippolyte and gifted to the victorious Wonder Woman. The queen also gives her daughter a name, which frankly seems long overdue, dubbing her Diana, after the goddess of the moon, who just happens to be the princess' godmother!

Much has already been said about Marston, his theories and philosophies, his unconventional throuple lifestyle, and his decidedly kinky inclinations, such as in the book *The Secret History of Wonder Woman*, by Jill Lepore, and the Hollywood film *Dr. Marston and the Wonder Women*. However, since these themes aren't the focus of this essay, I'm going to limit my references to only the most relevant points of contact between creator and creation.

Having noted that, the pervasive themes of bondage and submission that appear so frequently later in the run are in short supply in the debut story. There are the shackles they wear as bracelets to remind them to be wary of men's treachery, but that's about it. There's no real sign of it in the follow-up story in *Sensation Comics* #1, either, which unspools as follows:

While piloting Steve Trevor home in her transparent stealth plane, he regains consciousness just long enough to mistake Diana for an angel. Wonder Woman conceals her plane in a deserted barn and carries Trevor to the hospital. Moulton wastes no time establishing her great powers. In short order she defeats some bandits, outraces a car, and dangles a thieving theatrical promoter from an electrical pole.

Wonder Woman then returns to Trevor's hospital and encounters a nurse on the steps, sobbing over her wayward fiancé. She makes a quick deal with the nurse, who is her doppelgänger, and who also happens to be named Diana—Diana Prince. Wonder Woman buys the nurse's identity for a wad of cash, so the nurse can chase down her fiancé in South America.

Much Nazi thwarting ensues, allowing Steve Trevor and Wonder Woman to establish their freedom-fighting coalition, which seems to involve Diana rescuing Trevor time and again, although Trevor frequently proves he is a crack shot with a pistol and can throw a decent roundhouse. The episode ends with Trevor back in the hospital, now so fully enamored of Wonder Woman that he lobs this little gem at Diana Prince: "*Listen, Diana! You're a nice kid, but if you think you can hold a candle to Wonder Woman, you're crazy!*" And so, Diana Prince becomes her own rival in her pursuit of Trevor's love.

If there was anything about this origin story that truly surprised me, it's that Wonder Woman doesn't receive her magic lasso along with her weirdly patriotic culottes and eagle breastplate. I'd always thought it was part of the original outfit, but not so. The magic lasso doesn't appear until *Sensation Comics* #6, which also happens to be the issue that introduces the giant kangaroo mounts of the Amazons, possibly my all-time favorite element of the stories. By this time, the bondage themes are already in play. The first Kanga competition we see is a fun little game known as "girl-roping"!

Later in the issue, as a reward for her exceptional work in the world of men, Diana gets her magic lasso. It is forged by Amazon craftswoman Metala from the fine chains of Hippolyte's magic girdle. Aphrodite and Athena decree that anyone who is bound by the lasso must obey her commands, which would include telling the truth of course, but it should be noted that someone under the control of the lasso may also be forced to lie. This is demonstrated in *Sensation Comics* #13 when the villainess Olga gets the drop

93

on Wonder Woman with her own rope and forces her to confess to murdering a gang of crooks. The lasso can only make the truth known when it is wielded by someone with honorable intent.

With the addition of the magic lasso, all the fundamental elements of the Wonder Woman mythos are in place.

During wartime, the tales alternate between the thwarting of Nazis and their allies, (with all the usual unfortunate wartime stereotyping) and much more fanciful fare, like outer-space aliens, underground and underwater civilizations, and adventures through time.

Wonder Woman #1 - *Wonder Woman* # 45

In the first official issue of *Wonder Woman* a retelling of the origin story adds a lot of startling new information.

A strange parchment, dropped by Wonder Woman as she leaves Steve Trevor at an American hospital, offers a retelling of the origins of the Amazons which expands the story. We are introduced to Ares, the god of war, and his rivalry with the goddess Aphrodite. Armies of men, inspired by Ares's warlike ways, rule the world by the sword and treat its women as chattel. In response, Aphrodite sculpts a race of super women and breathes life into them. She again gifts Hippolyte with the magic girdle and the Amazons proceed to conquer Ares's armies.

Following this revelation, we get a recap of the treachery of Hercules from the first origin story, including the eventual redemption of the Amazons and the establishment of Paradise Island. Then we learn the startling fact that Diana was also sculpted by Hippolyte under the instruction of Athena and brought to life by Aphrodite.

One presumes this twist was added in consideration of the nagging question of how there could be any children at all on an island populated exclusively by immortal women. Without this clarification, one might jump to the conclusion that Paradise Island women with a yen for motherhood made the occasional excursion out into the world of men in search of suitable genetic material. Hey, what happens in Vegas, stays in Vegas, right? Juvenile Amazons do appear in the comic, though there is never confirmation that all Amazon girls are animated sculptures. In any case, sculpture Diana gets her name from Aphrodite this time around, rather than from her mother, and quickly grows into the greatest of all the Amazons.

This brings us to Steve Trevor's fateful crash landing on Paradise Island. A new wrinkle is also added to the narrative of Diana's nursing skills. In this version she develops a purple healing ray that literally brings him back to life.

Meanwhile, Mars/Ares taunts Aphrodite with his achievement of fomenting a second world war. The embarrassed goddess tasks Hippolyte with finding the strongest Amazon maiden to return Trevor to the fight, and act as their agent in the world of men. We get the same story of the contest (with giant kangaroos added) and Diana triumphs. She is gifted with her uniform, including the magic lasso, which explains my earlier confusion, and off she flies to the United States in her invisible airplane.

In this new run of the character, Mars, and his aides Greed, Deception, and Conquest become specific antagonists.

By this time, the themes of bondage, discipline, spanking, role playing, and even a little Furry action are well established. Many complaints and concerns were leveled by certain social activists and public figures, but Marston was utterly committed to his belief in the importance of discipline and submission as elevated human traits. However, later in his run, the bondage themes become so prevalent that they mar the storytelling. Wonder Woman is tied up with her own lariat or chained by her bracelets so often that it becomes rather tedious.

In 1945 Marston was diagnosed with cancer. During his illness, writing duties were gradually taken over by Joye Hummel, among others. A former student of Marston's, Hummel's stories retained the bondage and discipline content, though she did back away from the wall-to-wall frequency of it that marked Marston's former tenure on the book. This was all to the better, in my opinion, because it made for improved pacing and narrative interest.

However, after his death in 1947, Hummel left the title, and the kinky themes were further curtailed. One might say many things about Marston's writing; it was a tad corny and quippy, and he had a definite ideological axe to grind, but he did have a knack for keeping the action going. Some of the writing that followed him lacks the feeling of grand adventure he was able to evoke. Wonder Woman became, oddly, a bit of a matchmaker for young love, and short supporting features in the comic went from highlighting notable women from history to tips on dating, makeup, and marriage. The male editors and writers seemed unable, or unwilling, to identify with the character, falling back on "girly" romance content, to the general detriment of the magazine.

Another retelling of the origin in *Wonder Woman* #45 changed little, though some pains were taken to justify the oft-mentioned fact that the Amazons will lose their immortality if a man ever sets foot on Paradise Island. This, of course, conflicted with the fact the whole roller-coaster ride begins with Steve Trevor's airplane crash on the island. Diana finds a loophole, deciding he will never be allowed to touch the actual soil of the land. (This despite the fact he is clearly doing so in the fourth panel of the original *All-Star Comics* tale.) She therefore carries the injured airman to her laboratory, rather than the hospital of the earlier versions, and nurses him back to health while ensuring he never makes contact with the earth of Paradise Island.

Other small changes included Aphrodite herself leading the Amazons to Paradise Island, and a change of cast in the competition for the right to go into man's world. Unlike earlier versions, where Diana's friend Mala was the main rival, this version featured the huge Amazon Giganta as the last competitor. In previous incarnations, the bullets and bracelets competition was a two-person standoff. Here, the masked Diana faces off against no less than eight Amazons firing pistols at her, and still manages to fend off all bullets.

After the death of Marston, H. G. Peter continued to draw the strip, but, as the years rolled on, his style came to look a little old fashioned. The somewhat boyish, flapper's body type and bow lips were no longer in vogue. He continued to draw the interior pages, but he was eventually replaced as regular cover artist by the marvelous Irwin Hasen, who developed a more lithe, fashionable "Hollywood starlet" look for the character. After Peter's death in 1958, this hipper style for the interior art was continued by various stalwart DC artists.

Wonder Woman #98 is drawn by Ross Andru and inked by Mike Esposito and has a much more modern comics sensibility. There's more depth in the panels, more dynamic foreshortening, more variation of camera angle, stronger page design, and a more willowy, glamorous looking Diana.

The tale, written by Robert Kanigher, is deeply revisionist. No mention here of the history of the Amazons and their battle with Mars or Hercules, just an entreaty to Hippolyte from Pallas-Athena to choose the greatest of the Amazons for a mission into man's world to "*battle crime, injustice, and aid those in distress.*" This rather awkwardly excised all the dated World War II motivations, and replaced Aphrodite, the sexy goddess of love, with the brainier and more athletic Athena. Unlike previous retellings, Diana is already in her Wonder Woman garb rather than being gifted with it before her journey to man's world.

Diana isn't forbidden to join in the contest, but it is pointed out that the arbiter of the event, Hippolyte, might unintentionally favor her daughter. Diana's rather fanciful solution to the problem is to disguise the entirety of the competing Amazons as herself so her mother can't distinguish her daughter from the crowd. The Amazonian perruquers and tailors must have loved the all-nighter that resulted from that little royal decree. Diana wins the contest, as per usual, and is, rather outlandishly, tasked by Pallas-Athena to parley a single penny into a million dollars for children's charity.

Before Wonder Woman can get started on this philanthropic errand, the Amazons spot an airplane going down over the island. It's good old Steve Trevor, of course, plummeting toward the Earth because his parachute hasn't opened properly. Diana catapults herself into the sky, latches onto the airman, and uses her mighty breath to inflate the parachute and blow them, in short order, to— the coast of the United States! I know the location of Themyscira isn't clearly nailed down, but it seems surprisingly close to America in this narrative.

The remaining hijinks have little bearing on the origin story, but it's clear DC is groping for something outside the wartime beginnings of the character and the title's long-standing themes of bondage and discipline. I find this story rather less than compelling, and the silliness of it overrides the drama to a great degree. This isn't to say the Marston years lacked silliness and whimsical ideas, they certainly didn't, but there was a certain naive energy to the tales that created a charming foundation for the character's adventures. The changes here seem rather uninspired.

In the following issue Wonder Woman fends off Steve's insistence on a contest for her hand in marriage, and she ends up disguising herself as Diana Prince and becoming his secretary.

There's no doubt that much of this is written by men who have little feeling for the feminist roots of the character. For some time, her great power and bold independence had been fading, but at this point something truly vital goes out of the character.

Wonder Woman # 105

In a strange little episode entitled "The Secret Origin of Wonder Woman," a few truly inexplicable things occur. The baby Diana is visited in her bassinet by some gods and goddesses who endow her with gifts. Beauty and goodness from Aphrodite, all the wisdom of the planets (whatever that is) from Athena, incredible speed from Mercury, and great strength from—Hercules? One of the main villains of the first origin is treated like a gruff uncle here, with no hint of his former treachery.

Then, only a few panels later, we are treated to this bizarre tableau: In the foreground we see Hippolyte, sorrowful, her head in her hand, a scroll dangling from the other, and in the background several Amazons wailing in anguish.

> Caption: *Then, one bleak day, years later, terrible news...*
> Hippolyte: *All the men... wiped out... in the wars...!*
> Amazons: *Woe is us... we are... alone... now–!*

I mean, what the hell is this? Are we to presume the Amazons had both genders until the men were destroyed in the wars? It seems that way to me, despite that being against everything Marston wanted for the character. In their grief the widowed women are motivated to flee the wars and seek out a peaceful place of their own. The young Diana, dubbed Wonder Girl by her mother the queen, quickly cobbles together a ship and protects it from all manner of dangers as they sail the open seas. In the end they pass through some strange gasses and discover Paradise Island. Those gasses are, Athena tells them, the mists of eternal youth which will keep them all young so long as they stay on the island.

The Wonder Girl tales, perhaps an attempt to woo younger readers to the magazine, are added as a regular feature in the mag with #105, alongside yarns featuring Wonder Woman and the diminutive Wonder Tot. This long run, written by Bob Kanigher and drawn by Ross Andru and Mike Esposito, chronicles Wonder Girl and Wonder Tot's adventures on Paradise Island and other islands in the vicinity. Many stories center around the adolescent Amazon's bumpy romance with the amorous, fish-tailed Mer-Boy, and his continuing efforts to woo Wonder Girl at undersea sock-hops and soggy, submarine soda fountains. The "Impossible Tale" format is frequently in play, wherein all three ages of Wonder Woman are able to team up against some threat or other. It's not that the stories are entirely without charm, and Andru's terrific layouts make for pretty satisfying visuals, but the bulk of the feminist ideals of the earlier strip have been squeezed out of the equation. It's pretty thin gruel, all things considered.

And so it continues for some time to come, though startling changes were in the offing.

The Bronze Age: *Wonder Woman* # 179

DC went through some tough times in the 1960s. Their staid professionalism began to look pretty threadbare in comparison to hip upstart Marvel Comics. The realities of the business demanded DC make some effort to adapt. While young comics artists like Jim Steranko and Neal Adams were transforming the visual landscape of the industry, certain aspiring writers were attempting to do the same. One of those young mavericks was Denny O'Neil, and he was tasked with steering Wonder Woman into more groovy waters in 1969.

O'Neil severs all ties with the old origin of the character by having the Amazons zip off to another dimension to recharge their magical energies. Diana is asked to either accompany them or stay and relinquish her powers. Unable to abandon Steve Trevor, she opts to remain. The entire event is glossed over rather briskly, in only two pages of continuity. The island, along with Diana's Amazonian friends and mother, simply fades away and disappears from Earth. It's not exactly a revamping of her earlier origin, but it is a clear severance from that origin, to allow for a new approach.

In equally short order Diana meets, and begins to train with, her new martial arts sensei, I Ching. While not as egregious a depiction of Asians as in the wartime stories, I Ching still retains a touch of inconsistent patois, and a certain inscrutable Charlie Chan demeanor. This mysterious teacher from the East has his own agenda and he trains Diana for their mutual benefit. She seems to retain some residual Amazonian vigor which allows for single-minded focus and rapid mastery of several martial arts techniques. In no time she's out kicking butt in an effort to locate her wayward paramour, Steve Trevor.

Capitalizing on the popularity of the spy genre, and perhaps inspired by the character Emma Peel in the British TV series The Avengers, Diana is remolded into a covert spy. She goes up against a host of new villains, including Dr. Cylvia Cyber, a character reminiscent of Ian Fleming's Dr. No, bent on world domination, and commanding an all-girl gang. Diana even gets her own Q, a former criminal who provides her with an array of weaponized jewelry.

In *Wonder Woman* # 180 Steve Trevor is gunned down mercilessly, and while the event warrants depiction on the cover, Diana does little mourning over him in successive installments. Presumably, this is to open up other romantic possibilities, but it plays as a little cold blooded, especially since she chose to stay in man's world because of her love for him. Next, she opens a kicky fashion boutique as a cover, and prepares to battle any and all menaces to the American status quo.

In issues #183 and #184 Diana takes a trip back to Paradise Island, to help her mother battle Ares. In a startling turn of events, we learn that Ares is Hippolyte's father and Diana's grandfather. This counters the existing narrative that the Amazons, and Diana, were sculpted and brought to life by Aphrodite. The matter of the older rule, whereby any men occupying Paradise Island will cause the Amazons to lose their immortality and powers, is also brought into question, since there are literal armies of them in the episode. These bizarre changes were subsequently abandoned with extreme prejudice.

While the public reaction to the title's bold transformation was mostly negative, they are, in retrospect, pretty entertaining comics. Perhaps they aren't technically Wonder Woman comics, but the slick, illustrative art by Mike Sekowsky and Dick Giordano, and the breezy writing by O'Neil and others, make them quite readable.

But the new series was not beloved by much of the buying public. In the fallout from the negative response the new direction flounders about for a time, throwing random genres against the wall, tossing in reprints, generally unsure of what it wants to be. In 1972, feminist Gloria Steinem began lobbying for DC to reinstate Wonder Woman's powers. She did so, in part, by putting Wonder Woman on the first newsstand issue of Ms. Magazine and by generally shaming DC for removing her superhuman abilities.

Ultimately, the company leapt at the opportunity to dump the controversial new direction and returned Diana to her original roots.

Much like the perfunctory death of Steve Trevor, the demise of I Ching is quick and brutal, as he's shot down by a mad sniper terrorizing the city. It seems DC would brook little delay in getting back to the status quo, but they do take a moment for the first victim of the sniper to be named as Dottie Cottonman, women's magazine editor. One can only interpret this as a quick middle finger from the beleaguered editorial staff in response to Ms. Steinem's activist agenda.

In her efforts to stop the sniper from killing anyone else, Diana tumbles off a building and falls onto a projecting gargoyle, bringing on a bout of amnesia. Driven by some deep compulsion she abandons her hospital bed, steals a military jet, and heads for Paradise Island.

She manages to get there but has no memory of her mother or much of anything else. Luckily, the advanced technology of the Amazons has a solution, a quick zap from the Amazon Memory Bank, via an electronic headset. Before the procedure, however, Hippolyte admonishes the doctor to omit a few items from the download. Diana's memory is replenished, and we are reminded of the original story of the Amazons, though Steve Trevor's crash landing on the island is conspicuously absent.

Diana's status as Wonder Woman is then called into question by an armored Amazon warrior, who almost defeats her in battle. She is revealed as Nubia, a black Amazon, who lives on a nearby "floating island" concealed in the mists. Nubia vows she will one day prove she is the only true Wonder Woman. Hippolyte hints at some secret concerning the mighty, armored woman.

A slightly confused Diana is quickly dumped back in Washington DC and by using her knowledge of all Earth languages she secures a job as a UN guide. Her great feats of strength and daring are also reinstated, and she meets a new love interest, Morgan Tracy. Tracy, like Steve Trevor before him, falls for Wonder Woman and ignores Diana.

It's later revealed that Nubia was created right along with Diana, but was stolen in her infancy by Mars, and raised to be a warrior to help him exact his revenge on the Amazons. The two Wonder Women battle, but in the end, Nubia comes to embrace the Amazonian ideal of love over war.

After this the publishers take another left turn. Several subsequent issues are dedicated to retelling classic Moulton tales out of Wonder Woman's past, via the reading of some ancient scrolls. Artist Ric Estrada's bold, stripped-down art style effectively evokes an earlier age, but even though these are mighty fine comics in my opinion, it would be a short-lived interlude.

Post Crisis: *Wonder Woman* #1- 3 (Vol. 2)

George Perez, with the help of Karen Berger, Greg Potter, and Len Wein, seized the opportunity available in the wake of *Crisis on Infinite Earths* and returned Wonder Woman to her roots in Greek mythology in 1987. Other characters were also concurrently revamped, including Superman, by John Byrne, and Batman in the wake of Frank Miller's *The Dark Knight Returns*.

Perez, the main driver behind the entire WW enterprise, was at the height of his considerable powers, turning out beautifully rendered art and bravura storytelling. Perez and Potter did a deep, deep dive, recreating the origin story with a sweeping, operatic verve, adding greater detail and some wonderful new ideas.

There is unrest on Mount Olympus. Ares, reimagined here as an imposing Vader-esque figure in black armor, is dead-set against Artemis's intention to create a new race. She plans to generate a cadre of powerful women who would steer warlike mankind down a better path toward oneness with the gods. Ares believes mankind should simply be crushed and enslaved, while Artemis and Athena argue they should stay true to the hopes of lost Gaea. Zeus tires of the bickering and tells them to work it out amongst themselves. In the end, Ares relents, thinking his powers beyond all resistance.

Rather than the Amazons being shaped from clay and brought to life by the magic of the gods, Athena travels to the Cavern of Souls, the womb of Gaea, where the spirits of women who were unjustly murdered by men will act as animus for the creation of the Amazons. They are birthed as fully grown adults in the womb of a lake. Athena, Artemis, Hestia, and Aphrodite, each in turn, gift the Amazons with wisdom, skill in the hunt, a city to house them, and the great gift of love. Hippolyte is named queen, and Antiope her second, and they are each awarded a magic girdle, directly from Gaea.

In time, after a little underhanded prodding by Ares, Heracles is roused to great anger at Hippolyte, and he leads his legions to Themyscira (which is not on an island) to kick some ass. The ass that gets kicked is his own, of course, as Hippolyte proves to be more than his equal. Thus failed, Heracles falls back on subterfuge, pretending this was merely a test, to be certain the Amazons were worthy allies. This Heracles is somewhat more vindictive than the Hercules of the original Marston tales. He proceeds to poison and beat Hippolyte, steal her girdle as a prize, and, if we can take him at his word, to rape her while she is unconscious. A rather darker road than Marston would ever have traveled, I believe.

The chained Hippolyte begs the goddesses for forgiveness and is given a rap on the knuckles for straying from her mandated mission to lead mankind down a better path. Thus freed, the Amazons make quick, bloody work of Heracles' legions, but go too far. Antiope attempts to rouse them in pursuit of the retreating Heracles, but Hippolyte puts the kibosh on that plan, decreeing they must never again fight with vengeance in their hearts. Antiope cannot agree, so she relinquishes her magic girdle and rides away with her followers.

Later, Heracles is given a redemption, of sorts, apologizing to the Amazon nation, and mending the rift between he and Hippolyte, despite his desecration of her. In a somewhat challenging move, Hippolyte accepts his apology and even speaks of tender feelings toward him. Surprising, but perhaps in keeping with the Amazon mandate of love over hate and violence.

The goddesses decide the wayward Amazons must atone for their sins by overseeing the confinement of some ancient evil entombed in the heart of an island. They accept and build a city of beauty and culture on this island paradise.

Next, in echoes of the retelling in the earlier *Wonder Woman* #1, a strange urge grows within Hippolyte. She is informed that the spirit of the woman who acted as the spark of life for her was pregnant at the time of her death, and that the unborn child calls to her. She goes to the beach, sculpts a babe, and awaits the spirit of her unborn child to animate the sandy simulacrum. As the child's spirit flies from the Cavern of Souls several goddesses confer gifts upon her.

"I, Demeter, grant her power and strength, like that of the Earth itself!"

"I, Aphrodite, give her great beauty and a loving heart!"

"I, Athena, grant her wisdom!"

"I, Artemis, shall give her the eye of the hunter, and unity with the beasts!"

"I, Hestia, grant her sisterhood with fire, that it may open men's hearts to her!"

"I, Hermes, give her speed and the power of flight!"

Thus blessed, Diana is born and over the years grows to be the greatest of all Amazons. At this point, the oracle of the island, Menalippe, is given a terrible vision of trouble in man's world. She passes on a decree from the goddesses that a tournament must be held to select the greatest of all Amazons to go on a mission into the civilization beyond the island. Hippolyte forbids Diana from taking part, but this time, after appealing to the gods for a purpose in her life, a disembodied celestial voice assures Diana she shall have that purpose. Hidden, as are all the competitors behind the golden helmets of their armor, Diana gains her victory and is awarded silver bracelets to replace her iron ones.

Unfortunately, she must face one final trial: *The Flashing Thunder!*

The Paradise Island of this retelling seems to lack the technological advancements of Marston's version; without planes, pistols, or advanced medical equipment of their own, they have somehow come into possession of a .45 pistol. In a darker and grittier version of Bullets and Bracelets, Diana manages to thwart the slugs, but is amazed and appalled at the power of this strange new weapon.

I confess I was not a follower of the title during the Perez years, but this is top notch comics, beautifully illustrated, with superior storytelling, and filled with compelling drama. Some great Wonder Woman comics follow after this era, but I can't point to a run that I enjoyed reading more than this one.

Wonder Woman #101 (Vol. 2)

During John Byrne's 1995-1998 run on the title, things got a little convoluted. George Perez's revamping of the character, reimagining her as a newly minted hero, left a hole in the historical continuity, effectively wiping out her early WWII years, her role in the Justice Society of America, and complicated her relationship with Donna Troy.

Donna, known as Wonder Girl, has a complex history, beginning as a younger version of Diana herself, but later becoming an adopted sister who was rescued from a fire by Diana and taken to Paradise Island. After Perez's changes to the timeline Donna's origin transformed again; the sorceress Magala created a magical duplicate of Diana, but she was kidnapped by Dark Angel, who curses her to— well, it's all *very* complicated.

In an effort to reestablish the pre-Crisis tales as canon, and sort out the Donna Troy conundrum, Byrne built a Byzantine justification.

It began with Diana's death.

After being destroyed by the demon Neron, the empty husk of Diana's body lays in a hospital, but J'onn J'onzz uses his psychic ability to confirm that her soul is still out there, somewhere, suffering endless pain. To make a long story short, she eventually expires, all due to a spell Hippolyte had Magala cast upon Diana in hopes of avoiding her death. The good news is, Diana is reborn as a straight-up goddess. The Goddess of Truth.

On Themyscira, Hippolyte's crime of meddling with fate is met with this judgment: She will take Diana's place in the world as Wonder Woman. Meanwhile, an aging Jay Garrick, the first Flash, gets a funny feeling about Hippolyte as Wonder Woman, and they both abscond into the past of World War II to check it out. Hippolyte eventually decides to stay and fight the Nazis, bringing all the Golden Age stories back into continuity. One might say this doesn't technically countermand Diana's origin, but if those original tales were in fact experienced by Hippolyte rather than Diana, I feel it's relevant.

Byrne saves one last revelation for the end of his run. Ares reveals that the pregnant spirit from the Well of Souls who became Hippolyte was his own daughter, and that Diana is his granddaughter, making her a direct descendant of Zeus. However, since the newly minted goddess Diana has been meddling in human affairs, contrary to Olympian law, she is once again banished to Earth to take up the mantle of Wonder Woman.

The Byrne run is rife with very athletic narrative contortions beyond just Hippolyte's time-traveling, including Wonder Girl and her powers, her curse, and her very existence, a strange composite Zeus who adopts the moniker "Jove," and lots of Kirby-inspired storylines including the New Gods, Darkseid, the Demon, and more. Honestly, it all becomes a bit much. Though I am a fan of Byrne's career as a whole, there was a certain deterioration in his art at this stage of the game. He was never his own best inker, in my opinion, and the art here comes off as somewhat rushed, in both the quality of the drawing and the page design. It's solid, but not as fresh and engaging as some of his earlier efforts with top-notch embellishers in play. Adding to this the many strained narrative developments (there are no fewer than four "Wonder Womans" in the run) and it all comes across as a little ham-fisted. There's still a lot of entertainment value here, but having read them once I doubt I'd return for a second perusal.

Wonder Woman #145 (Vol. 2)

New writer Eric Luke, without changing the specifics of the origin of Wonder Woman, added a strange new coda in 1999. Even as Hippolyte walks away from the beach with her newborn child, Cronus, father of Zeus, creates a second child from the clay of Themiscyra's shore. Cronus has his children afford the child with gifts, in a mockery of the goddesses' gifts to Diana.

"I, Disdain, give the beauty to control emotion, to become the perfect woman to send man to her will."

"I, Arch, give the mind of a cunning strategist."

"We, Titan, bestow the power of the earthquake."

"I, Slaughter, give her the precision of the killer, the knowledge of painful death."

There is only silence of thought as Oblivion gives her the ability to walk men's memory.

"I, Harrier, give the speed of flight, fastest if for the kill."

"I, Cronus, give her the gift of life and the name that shall sunder the world... Devastation."

It's a strong concept, to create a sort of Anti-Wonder Woman to serve as her evil counterpart, and it's played out well by Luke and artist Matthew Clark. Cronus and his children continue to vex Diana even after the defeat of Devastation, all this enclosed within the astounding covers of Adam Hughes's tenure as cover artist. Luke had a real sense of Wonder Woman's innate nobility and goodness, and while he pushed the boundaries of how far she might go in her quest for peace, he never lost sight of her foundation. He also did some intriguing things with the idea of Diana's psychically linked airplane. Very readable comics, overall.

The New Millennium: 2000 -2010

Though Eric Luke's run continued into the year 2000, the reins were soon handed over to writer-artist Phil Jimenez. As a fan of the Perez years, Jimenez acted as a keeper of the flame, making no significant changes to the origin, and maintaining the grandeur, operatic tone, and Olympian focus of the Perez run. After that, Gail Simone took over the writing and generally maintained the status quo, though she did add one small twist. The clay Hippolyte used to sculpt her daughter may have been infused with the essence of Cottus, a primordial son of Gaea. Near the end of Gail's run, the creature is released by the vengeful Amazon warrior Alkyone, but Cottus is defeated by Zeus's lightning exploding from Diana's bracelets. It is also worth noting that during this era the thorny question of romantic love on an island without men is tacitly, if not explicitly, confirmed.

All-New Wonder Woman

Slumming TV writer J. Michael Straczynski takes an extreme left turn, creating an entirely new timeline in which to explore his particular variation on the Wonder Woman mythos. Straczynski, along with artists Don Kramer and Phil Hester, begin their exploration of this bent reality with a young Diana, wearing an all-new outfit (designed by Jim Lee) and battling "Men in Black" styled assassins. As she battles, Diana laments her lack of knowledge about who she is, who she's fighting, and why. After the assassins' attempt to kill Diana with a suicide bomb fails, Diana returns home, which is a sewer full of robed and hooded figures, apparently, and demands to see the oracle, Menalippe. The oracle provides Diana with a vision of the ruins of her former Paradise Island home, and how it was destroyed.

In the Straczynski version Aphrodite has summarily removed her protection from Themyscira and its Amazonian inhabitants. As a consequence, men, led by a mysterious silhouetted figure, arrive to destroy them. In desperation, Hippolyte sends many Amazons, including her daughter, out into the world. She then commits her remaining troops to one final, glorious, battle to the death. The mysterious figure questions the defeated Hippolyte with the irresistible magic lasso, but to avoid giving up the location of her daughter, Hippolyte flings herself into a fire and takes her own life.

The Oracle then informs Diana that this version of reality is somehow false. "*The past you saw... isn't the past that was... and we have to put it right...*" Diana vows to kill them all.

Forces are still trying to destroy the surviving Amazons scattered throughout the world and Diana comes to their defense. This is a young, but bitter Diana, a defiant Diana, who kills without remorse and openly challenges the vague will of the gods. With an Amazonian sword, and a new shield bearing her mother's likeness, she goes about systematically destroying her enemies.

Eventually her enemies are revealed as the Morrigan, a triune of three goddesses: the Celtic Anann, the Roman Bellona, and the Greek Enyo. The mysterious figure of the earlier issues is their agent, a former soldier and torturer, who fights Diana to a standstill, but who is eventually undone. These enemies are window dressing, however. Yet another evil entity lurks behind these many malefactors.

You've gotta give Straczynski his props here; this is a clever way of reimagining the character because the altered timeline has a built-in "out." He can do anything, recreate any villain, kill off any character, and once the twisted reality is corrected the Wonder Woman title can go right back to its normal state of affairs. In the middle of the series Dr. Psycho shows Diana multiple dimensions, wherein she always becomes a crusader for justice of one sort or another, teasing many more tales that might be told. Straczynski ultimately returned Diana to her true reality, but his time on the title was short-lived. DC soon whisked him off to other projects, delivering the book to a new team, for yet another new direction.

Brian Azzarello and Cliff Chiang embraced their inner Goths and recreated the Wonder Woman mythos with a darker, somewhat more sordid, reality in 2011. When Zola, a human woman, is found to be impregnated by Zeus, his slighted spouse, Hera arrives to destroy her and the unborn child. Rescued by a reimagined, bird-footed Hermes, and given a magic key, Zola is transported to Wonder Woman's side. Diana takes on the role of Zola's protector and decides to hide her on Paradise island. Strife, a legitimate daughter of Hera and Zeus, arrives in Themyscira to cause general mischief and also to let a certain cat out of the bag by referring to Diana as her sister.

Hippolyte is forced to confess that Diana was not made from clay but was the offspring of her illicit love affair with Zeus. She fled with her child and to help secure their safety Zeus did not follow. The tale of Diana being formed from clay and animated by the goddesses was concocted to keep the vengeful Hera from destroying the baby Diana. Diana storms off in a huff, taking Zola, Strife, and Hermes with her back to the outside world. Soon Diana regrets her temper but returns to find Hera has been busy. She has turned Hippolyte to stone and transformed the Amazons into snakes.

Other dark revelations became known during this run, including the answer to the burning question of how the Amazons manage to reproduce without any male presence on the island. In this retelling, the women warriors of Themyscira sail by night, board ships at sea, and have their way with willing seamen. Willing, that is, until after the act. In the fashion of the black widow spider, the Amazons destroy their seafaring lovers after consummation. The female offspring are kept in paradise, and the unwanted males are traded to a kind-hearted Hephaestus in return for weapons. Hephaestus gives these discarded boys lives of meaning in service to his forge.

Meanwhile, Zeus seems to have left the realm, or perhaps been murdered, and kingship of the gods is there for the taking. Hera assumes control, but Apollo, War, Poseidon, Hades, and others have their own claims to the throne.

I missed these comics entirely at the time, partly because I was getting rather fatigued with endless crossovers and recurring reimaginings of both the DC and Marvel universes. While I feel this run offers a rather cynical take on the origin, and perhaps dwells unduly on the horrific elements of the mythos, it fits nicely into the prevailing zeitgeist of the time, and is effectively told by Azzarello, Chiang, and others.

However, despite an impressive sales spike off the top, the New 52 numbers subsequently plummeted. Public reaction and reviews were polarized, and within months, DC went into damage control mode. The fresh ideas of the New 52 were, for better or worse, eventually countermanded in toto.

Rebirth

In the 2016 Rebirth series, post *Flashpoint*, Greg Rucka alternated between two timelines, one in the present and one a flashback to Wonder Woman's origin, where Rucka offers a somewhat massaged version of the usual touchstones. Retooled without the World War II baggage, a young adult Diana longs to know the world beyond her utopian island home. The next day, while exploring a decaying tree she has never before seen, Diana is bitten by a poisonous snake. After her recovery, a crack team of American warriors led by Steve Trevor crash-lands on Themyscira. All die with the exception of Trevor himself. The lingering idea of no men being allowed to set foot on the island is unceremoniously countermanded, as is the ability of the Amazons to speak all the languages of the world. Nevertheless, they nurse the wounded Trevor back to health.

In a change from the Perez years, the Amazons are somewhat less directly connected to their patron gods and goddesses than before, and as they consider the strange accouterments (including the guns) of the American warriors, they seek to find and interpret symbolic messages from the gods. This seems like a clear attempt to move away from the grand Olympian drama that dominated the title for so many years. The snakebite Diana received at the tree, now referred to as

"The Gate," the entrance to Themyscira, is interpreted as proof that Ares is meddling in the world of men and that he is part of the plan of the gods. Therefore, they must choose a champion to accompany Trevor back into his outside reality. Unlike earlier versions, Hippolyte sees Diana's victory in the upcoming games as predestined, but tries, unsuccessfully, to talk her out of competing anyway.

Diana wins her way into the final three contestants. Here Bullets and Bracelets is reimagined as a necessary skill for survival in the outside world of guns and only Diana is able to successfully parry the projectiles. Awarded the new armor of a victorious warrior and the souped-up magic lasso, renamed "The Golden Perfect" which allows Diana to meet with people in a sort of "truth-limbo," amongst other things. Steve and Diana then board his own plane, retrofitted with Amazonian invisibility technology, and off they fly.

In man's world, unable to communicate, and in spite of Trevor's entreaties, Wonder Woman is incarcerated. It is there in her jail cell, and not on Themyscira, that the gods appear to Diana in the guise of animal avatars, and dole out their great gifts of strength, speed, wisdom, and more. One additional small difference: In this version Diana cannot return to Themyscira, because she doesn't know how to do so. In this reality, she can never go home.

Thus, Rucka essentially returns the character to her pre-New 52 status, with little reference to, or tears shed, for what went before. There is some great art here by Liam Sharp, Nicola Scott, Bilquis Evely, and others, but I confess I'm not particularly enamored with Greg Rucka's writing. His ideas are intriguing enough, but I find his execution wordy and often preachy, and jam-packed with a great number of weak attempts at humor. Still, the new structure, with respect for the history of the origin, set the foundation for what will follow.

What Remains

In 2017, Rucka is followed by Shea Fontana, who sticks with the program, and James Robinson, who mostly does the same, though he did conjure a long-lost brother for Diana. It was twins for Hippolyte and Zeus, it seems, and while a girl-child was easily hidden amongst the Amazons the baby boy, Jason, was sent into man's world to be raised by the former Argonaut, Glaucus and be trained by his half-brother, Hercules.

More writers followed: G. Willow Wilson, Steve Orlando, Mariko Tamaki, Michael W. Conrad and Becky Cloonan. They teamed with lots of talented artists, such as Cary Nord, Mikel Janin, Marcio Takara, and many more. Wonder Woman battles a host of menaces, old and new, winning her way to victory through guile, strength, and loving understanding, and eventually finds her way back to Themyscira. She even dies again, ascends to Olympus again, and once again refuses godhood so she can return to Earth.

But, up until the closing of this essay, there are no further notable revisions to the essentials of her origin story. I'm sure there are more fresh takes on the horizon, but that ends the adventure as far as this particular document is concerned.

The More Things Change…

If there is one thing this essay has made clear, it is the truth of the old French adage: "*Plus ça change, plus c'est la même chose.*" En Anglais: "*The more things change, the more they stay the same.*" While Wonder Woman's history has included many versions, variations, and outright revampings, there seems to be an irresistible gravitational pull that inevitably returns the title to something resembling its first iteration. It is a compelling origin, one difficult to improve upon, and it's easy to see why it generally wins back its dominance. And, it must be said, the readers of comics do tend to resist change of any sort. I guess I'm one of those, because, despite enjoying some of the variations a great deal, I was always relieved to see them shift back to her traditional beginnings. If that outs me as an intractable Fanboy, I suppose I'll have to live with that. But, hey, I gotta be me!

Who are you?

The research and writing of this essay has been a strange and enlightening journey. As old as I am (and I'm really getting up there, folks), I do not date back to the 1941 debut of Wonder Woman. I have never before scanned every issue of a title that has been around for so long. Even with my favorite characters there have been times where I didn't follow the mag, for one reason or another. While I certainly can't claim to have perused every single issue of *Wonder Woman* and *Sensation Comics* in explicit detail, I have at least skimmed each one, and absorbed the overall gist of the story. And, of course, this only includes the run of the Wonder Woman title, proper. There are many other adventures for Diana, in the Justice League comics, various crossovers, Elseworlds, and scores of other titles I have never so much as laid eyes on.

It's an enlightening process, watching the changes in the way comic book stories are told, and how they reflect or anticipate the transformations of the world around them. In the beginning I experienced a character intended to embody a message of equality for women which was nonetheless mired in the prevailing sexism of the era. I immersed myself in the earnest but naive tales of wild fantasy and wartime battles against fascism but noted the casual racism that attended them. I enjoyed the cartoony rendering and the fanciful settings, but also witnessed Marston's overindulgent use of his personal obsessions. I observed the whitewashing and sterilization that followed in the wake of his powerful personality, and the virtual elimination of his overt feminist manifesto.

I watched as the quaint art and writing of the earlier issues gave way to more dynamic posing and page design and noted how attempts to modernize the character were often received with mixed or negative responses from the audience. I saw the character flounder through the late Seventies and into the Eighties, as the art once again began to look old-fashioned, and the stories eschewed the roots of the character, and then saw her gloriously renewed near the end of the decade. I observed, rapt, as the nature of the stories matured, and how the art became gradually more sophisticated and compelling. I became aware that the feminist message of Dr. Marston was allowed to flower once again, and in a much more illuminated manner than a man of his time could easily have imagined. I saw how even his belief in loving submission and fluid sexuality returned to the book, in a more refined and enlightened form, and how the caretakers of the property still maintained the magic, mayhem, and sweeping adventure he always brought to the title.

The way comics are made and how we consume them has also changed. Writers no longer bang away on typewriters, instead typing into digital programs and communicating with their artists and editors through emails and texts. Many artists have replaced pencil, paper, and ink with digital tablets and graphics software, delivering pages to secure file sharing sites. I read most of these comics through digital means of one sort or another, and that, too, has had a major effect on how we experience the art form. And I believe it is an art form, despite what some cynics might say. It may be that the medium has only rarely achieved its full potential, but there is always that enticing possibility.

I can't say all these Wonder Woman comics were great, by any means, nor that I enjoyed them all, or that I always found that elusive overlap between myself and Diana that allowed me to relate to her and her adventures. But, man, there's some very good stuff here if you have the time and inclination to peruse such a vast history of the character.

I hope some of you will.

Sam Agro is a cartoonist, writer, illustrator, and sometime performer. He creates storyboards for both live-action and animated media, including such projects as *Paw Patrol, Bunsen is a Beast, Fly Away Home*, and several installments of the *SAW* movie franchise. He also dabbles away at the fringes of the comic book industry and is a frequent essayist on pop culture subjects. Sam makes his home in Toronto with his wife, Beth, and their neurotic cat, Little V.

THE FANTASTIC FOUR

First Appearance: *Fantastic Four* #1, August 8th 1961

Tripping the Infinite Fantastic

By Thomas Deja

The first comic book anyone ever bought me was *Fantastic Four* #105.

My parents bought it for me at a corner candy store on Fresh Pond Rd. here in Queens, New York as a reward for being such a trooper at Dr. Sferraza's. I had a pretty good idea who the characters were from watching the Hanna Barbera cartoon—although there was this strawberry blonde girl with a funny hair clip that seemed to react as most people would react to a New York City street vendor hot dog circa 1970 that I didn't recognize, and the crackling energy bad guy (imaginatively named "Monster") didn't appear a lot after this...

...but the reason I bring this up is because this issue contained a summary of the Fantastic Four's origin. It does not end my association with the title; after all, I'm here talking to you about the team for a reason. One of the first comics I ever bought with my own money from another corner candy store across from my childhood home on Norwood Avenue in Brooklyn was *Fantastic Four* #137. That issue featured a really neat *kaiju* with a satellite for a head called "Warhead" on the cover. I was nuts for *kaiju* at that time, so the decision was an easy one to make. Granted, the story was a strange Roy Thomas mish-mash of nostalgia and continuity patches, but it prompted me to start collecting the series for the first time, something I would do off and on throughout my life.

Here in the 21st century, we all know the bullet points. Reed Richards, his fiancé Sue Storm, her brother Johnny, and Reed's best friend Ben Grimm go on an unscheduled rocket ship trip. They barely reach space when the quartet are bombarded with cosmic rays, altering their basic DNA until they are more than human. They crash-land somewhere and vow to defend humanity as the Fantastic Four.

What's interesting about the origin of Marvel's first family is that it's one of those origins that not only evolves over time but *must* evolve due to the very nature of the story. That original tale was so tied into both what was considered high tech and what was considered current events at the time that it demanded future retellings that adjusted it to keep up with advances in time and technology.

In 1961, that experimental rocket was designed to reach the moon ahead of those darn Russkies, and the four used their powers as...explorers. But then, 1961 Stan Lee wanted to do anything *but* imitate the Justice League of America, the original remit given to him by publisher Martin Goodman. In the fiftieth anniversary issue, *Fantastic Four* #358 (*Boy*, are you and I going to get back to that issue soon enough...), Marvel published some notes that came out of Lee's initial talks with Jack Kirby where our original iteration of the four were supposed to have their powers in a permanently "on" state—Sue had to wear a porcelain mask so everyone else could see where she was, and it took a while for Reed to pull himself back together after using his elasticity. Given Lee's desire to buck superhero conventions at the time, it's logical that Kirby, who had been ousted at DC from penciling a book he co-created, *Challengers of The Unknown*, would introduce the idea that the FF were to be adventurers in the more classic sense, searching to expand the boundaries of human knowledge. And if they were going to be adventurers, they wouldn't need special costumes or anything, would they? And even when the publisher demands there be costumes, they'll be simple uniforms just as likely to be work clothes as they could be costumes.

Another thing to consider is the insistence that the Marvel Universe happened "outside your front window." There was a definite sense of Marvel heroes, including the FF, happening *now* due to a succession of references to current events. Sometimes that would blow up in their face—that time the Thing wore a Beatles wig to meet his musical idols did date pretty rapidly when that group began to evolve away from their skiffle origins. I also don't think anyone brought up Reed's tour of duty with the OSS alongside Nick Fury during WWII after it was brought up in the twenty-first issue where they fought Masked Hitler, but for a while they kept this up. Young me remembers picking up *Fantastic Four* #178 ("Call My Killer The Brute," 1976), written by Roy Thomas and drawn by the amazing George Perez, and having the intrigue of the Frightful Four and its new member, the Brute—

You remember the Brute, right? That alternative version of Reed from Counter-Earth, an exact copy of our Earth created by the High Evolutionary...you know what? Doesn't matter right now to our talk.

—interrupted by a page where then-mayor of New York Abe Beame calls up Jimmy Carter, Gerald Ford, and Ronald Reagan looking for help a week before the 1976 election. This evoked a sense of awe in young me, because these were *real people* who might actually have *real* conversations in the Real World.

Throughout the period after Lee and Kirby left, where the book ping-ponged back and forth between Roy Thomas and Gerry Conway and Marvel went through what appeared to be its entire bullpen in an attempt to fill the position of editor in chief, the origin remained steady with the four aiming to reach the moon.

The first person who decided to tinker with the origin was Marv Wolfman. Wolfman was pretty stressed due to Jim Shooter taking the role of Editor-In-Chief at the time. He had also picked up the book from Len Wein in the middle of an epic arc that saw the team broken up because of Reed's power loss. This resulted in Wolfman penning solo stories for each member that were...less than stellar. Marv immediately began putting the group back together almost immediately, although *Fantastic Four* #197 ("The Riotous Return of the Red Ghost!" 1978) is primarily a Reed solo story, and apparently

Marv used it to address something that bugged the hell out of him.

In this issue, a powerless Reed recreates the accident that gave the FF powers thanks to funding from the naggingly familiar head of Cynthian Associates (the guy's a clone of Doctor Doom, who Doom is planning to infuse with the powers of the FF and take over the world by possessing the minds of the United Nations delegates, which I guess is more proof that Marvel Comics and clones never mixed). During his flight, we're treated to an interior monologue that sets out the new normal. To wit:

"It's taken years to prove my hunch—that the Cosmic Rays that showered us were slightly altered by heightened sunspot activity, by a flaring of the Van Allen Belt. There was even abnormal neutron activity that fateful day we became the FF. It was a chain of events that were repeated once since that time. And if I can recreate every link of that chain precisely—then Mister Fantastic will live once again!"

Wolfman wanted to very much acknowledge that we'd been to the moon and back several times without transforming astronauts into superhumans. What strikes me is how he seemed to overcompensate by throwing in all these extenuating circumstances. Maybe if he had made it only a flaring of the Van Allen Belt or sunspot activity that changed the cosmic rays, we would be building our future retcons on this one, but Wolfman slathered all of these factors onto the simple framework of the origin in this breathless manner and hopes for the best. Of course, Reed's experiment in Quantum Rube Goldberging does restore his abilities just in time for a fight with The Red Ghost, resplendent in his Disco Era outfit, complete with gold medallion bouncing on his exposed chest.

The 70's was a powerful drug.

To be fair, this is not a world shaking retcon. It's more of a recalibration to keep the classic origin plausible in light of the real-world events that followed it. It may not have been world shaking, but it was *necessary* to keep that "world outside your window" aesthetic alive. Wolfman moved on to introduce some forgettable characters (remember Willie "Doppelganger" Evans?), struggle with the presence of H.E.R.B.I.E. in the single season TV cartoon adaptation by De-

Pate-Feeling and incorporate characters from his just-canceled comic *Nova* in what was supposed to be a crossover. His original penciler Keith Pollard was also replaced by Canadian superstar John Byrne.

By this time, in the 80's, the Marvel policy of being "the world outside your window" made it clear that some of the facts this universe was built on had to be tweaked. It also didn't help that someone—maybe Jim Shooter at the same time he disposed of that pesky "reserved character" list?—instituted the Marvel Sliding Timeline, the idea that the current Marvel comics were happening at the time of release, and all the earlier issues happened within a set amount of years before that. I'm not sure, but I think the original MSL was seven years, but keep in mind that Marvel didn't even acknowledge the Timeline until the 00's, so actual facts may be muddied with the smudges of rumor and hearsay.

And Byrne...Byrne would come back in after a bit, and *boy*, did he have some things to say about the origin.

Fantastic Four #220 ("...And The Lights Went Out All Over the World," 1980) was the artist's first go at writing as well as penciling Marvel's First Family. This and the next issue were expanded from what was intended to be a promotional giveaway comic, and as such, it's a little generic while also giving us a hint at what would become one of the definitive runs in the title's history. After a sequence of scenarios showing our foursome individually helping people during a city-wide power outage—a sequence that reflects the opening sequence of the very first issue while also being unique in and of itself—and cameos by the Avengers and a member of Alpha Flight, we get Ben recounting the FF's origin...

"*That first flight the four of us took years ago, we rode in a different rocket then...a rocket specially designed by Reed to test his new star drive....a rocket that wasn't ready for its maiden flight.*"

So right out of the gate, Byrne had dispensed with the moon race rationale for that fateful flight and had shifted the need for the flight from national pride to Reed's hubris and ego. Ben elaborates further:

"*Reed was convinced that we had to sneak a flight before an appropriations cutback, and Sue and Johnny came along to prove how safe the drive was.*"

Okay, so maybe the hubris wasn't *exclusively* Reed's in this version. Hell, Ben implies there's an abundance of hubris all around for our quartet:

"We all knew the ship wasn't shielded well enough. We thought we knew the risks."

This last bit was kind of interesting in that it's the first time a writer does something that out and out contradicts the original origin story—Ben's words about accepting the risks do not jibe with the scene where he opposed the flight due to fear of cosmic rays. That won't be addressed until literally decades down the line...but we'll get to that in due time.

Young Me remembers reading this issue, which was dumped right in the middle of the ill-advised Doug Moench/Bill Sienkiewicz run (don't remember it? There's a good reason for that.) and ascribed this updating to making the origin less "specific" and more modern. That was definitely there, but I think there's another motive for this tweak.

You see, this is the first time a version of the origin put some shade on Reed Richards, but then, perceptions of Reed changed as the 70's rolled around and some good ol' paranoia about authority figures was setting in. Roy Thomas, who had taken over for Stan Lee, had Reed and Sue experience marital problems that results in a separation between the two starting in *FF* #130 ("Battleground: The Baxter Building, 1973). The writer who followed Thomas threw a little gas on the fire when Gerry Conway had Reed shut down his own son's mind to prevent his powers from fully manifesting (*FF* #141, "The End of The Fantastic Four," 1973—which incidentally contains main villain Annihilus recounting the original version of the FF's origin). It seems that Reed was now looked upon suspiciously by the next batch of writers, and Byrne embraced that blowback in 1980 when he put a lot more responsibility onto the Big Brain's back with this version. Yeah, there's that line about "we all knew the risks," but this version of the origin makes it clear that the flight was Reed's idea, was pushed forward by Reed's fear of defunding, and that Reed knew the rocket wasn't ready. We will see this emphasis on Reed being a Science Jerk increase as time goes on.

Byrne wasn't quite finished with the FF, as he took over as writer/penciller with *FF* #232 ("Back to the Basics," 1981). In that issue Byrne used the alchemical villain Diablo to imply that our heroes had been transformed along the lines of the four classic elements, with Reed repping Water, Sue Air, Johnny Fire, and Ben Earth. Four issues later for their 20th anniversary (*FF* #236, "Terror In A Tiny Town," 1981), Byrne opened with a dream sequence that showed us Johnny's point of view of the origin. It adjusted things a little bit, doubling down on the "star drive" explanation while also restoring Ben's misgivings about the flight. Another dream sequence showed us the confrontation in the very first issue with a number of new details to go with the star-drive angle—namely that even though there is some government funding involved that is in danger of being cut, most of the project has been financed by Reed's private fortune. The rest of the story, involving the Puppet Master, Doctor Doom, and "synthe-clones" (What did I tell you about clones and Marvel? There's even one hanging around this scenario of Doom named "Vincent Vaughn"...yes, really!) doesn't touch upon the origin, but Byrne's changes stood even after our heroes were back in the real world.

Byrne, even at this early date in his writing career, liked to tinker with established facts to line up with what he believed in, but for the rest of his run his origin tinkering was confined to filling in details. In *FF* #245 ("Childhood's End," 1982), it's mentioned that the site of the rocket crashing to earth was Ithaca, NY. In *FF* #269 ("Skyfall," 1984), we learn that Reed met Sue when he rented a room in her aunt's house while attending college, and that Sue was thirteen at the time when Reed was twenty...another little detail that will not age well and prompt someone to do a corrective down the line. In *FF* #271 ("Happy Birthday, Darling," 1984), we learn that the rocket was built by The Richards Rocket Group, and that Reed was inspired by an encounter with a giant alien invader named Gormuu to speed up the rocket launch ahead of the government's schedules.

Byrne's run ended with *FF* #293 ("Central City Does Not Answer," 1986), which started a story that was wrapped up by Roger Stern and Jerry Ordway over the next two issues.

The following issue (*FF* #296, "Homecoming," 1986) marks the first time a fact from the Byrne origin gets retconned...although Jim Shooter and Stan Lee's claiming the rocket crashed in Stockton, California and not Ithaca, New York could be ascribed to those two gentlemen neither knowing or caring about the details Byrne spent so long to set up. The issue commemorates the twenty-fifth anniversary of *Fantastic Four* #1 and recounts that first issue's events. Another walk back of Byrne's origin was Steve Englehart's having Sue refer to the purpose of the rocket flight as an attempt to win the space race in *FF* #326 ("The Illusion," 1989). To be fair, though, Englehart's time on the book was very unhappy. Originally brought in to "shake up" the status quo, which he did by jettisoning Reed and Sue in favor of Johnny's ex-girlfriend Crystal and what was at that time the current iteration of Ms. Marvel, who had been hanging out in Ben's solo series before it was canceled, he was quickly hamstrung by editorial interference. So, whether this reversion back to 1960s canon is because Steve either didn't care or was actively malicious in waiting out his contract, I can forgive it.

(You think I'm joking, but Englehart freely admits on his website, steveenglehart.com, that he was so discouraged by the demands of editorial that his last few issues—written under the pseudonym "John Harker"—feature clones made by a rogue Watcher and not the *actual* FF. What did I tell you about Marvel and clones?)

The origin resisted being adjusted throughout Walt Simonson's run as writer/penciller, a run where Simonson seemed primarily interested in amusing himself to the delight of the readers. But that origin, as well as a few other things that were established since the Lee-Kirby days, got shaken up something fierce three issues after new writer Tom DeFalco took over.

DeFalco was serving as Editor-In-Chief at Marvel at this time, taking over after the firing of Jim Shooter in 1987, and he had a certain vision for the company. Apparently, DeFalco did not care for the way Shooter had changed the face of the Marvel Universe during the

80s and decreed that all the titles had to revert back to their "classic" formation in anticipation of the company going public. The influence of DeFalco's Back To Basics plan was felt as early as Steve Englehart's run (and could arguably be the cause of the migration of a number of writers and artists to DC at the time, most significantly *X-Men*'s Chris Claremont), and when the flagship title of the company became free, he decided to handle it himself and turn it into an example of what he wanted...whether the reading public wanted it or not.

Fantastic Four #358 ("Whatever Happened To Alicia?" 1991) was the third issue of his run as well as the issue marking the book's fiftieth year of publication and it's one big retcon walking back the long-running story arc that saw Johnny date and ultimately marry Ben's former girlfriend Alicia, claiming she was a Skrull spy posing as Alicia ever since the first Secret Wars. A back-up story in the same issue ascribes something Simonson had planned to explore about Dr. Doom as just a misinformation campaign. Hidden in amongst all this was Reed recounting the origin, and DeFalco's version makes it clear that the object that brought the four into space wasn't a rocket...

"I *had designed a* starship *which could travel through hyperspace to other solar systems.*"

Yep...the rocket with a star drive was now upgraded to a starship with what amounted to a hyperdrive. And if that wasn't enough, the whole "sunspot activity altering the Van Allen Belt" elaboration of the cosmic rays that Marv Wolfman came up with was removed. It's almost as if DeFalco was intent on stripping things back to the Way It Was but threw us a tweak that helped perpetuate the World Outside Your Window trope. When you take into account the general rearranging of the deck chairs that made up this issue (I haven't even mentioned how the Puppet Master, who was kind of rehabilitated by Byrne and Roger Stern in their issues, did a full heel turn), it made DeFalco's run all the stranger given its emphasis on new opponents, a changing roster and sudden, whiplash-like change.

Maybe all the new characters were explained by Marvel's then-recent decision to give royalties to the character creators, which led to...well, DeFalco not making much. No one was waiting with bated breath for the return or use elsewhere of the likes of Dreadface, Wild Blood, Wild Streak, Lord Oculus, or Hyperstorm. Hell, the minute Marvel canceled the spin-off book *Fantastic Force*, none of those original characters were ever seen again except Vibraxas, who Christopher Priest co-opted during his exceptional run on *Black Panther* in the '00s.

DeFalco did touch upon the origin again amidst the near incoherent mess of *FF* #400. In the back-up tale, "In Memoriam," Ben, Johnny, and Sue reminisce about their origin in the most general tones, with even some of the updates the writer made left out. In the main story, "Even the Watchers Can Die," however, it's mentioned only in passing that Sue's powers came from her tapping into hyperspace...something that is dropped almost immediately afterwards.

All of that stuff DeFalco and artist Paul Ryan were setting up reaching back to the beginning of the run suddenly got dropped in 1996. Looking to boost sales of some of its core titles, Marvel entrusted them to Jim Lee and Rob Liefeld for the Heroes Reborn experiment. Nowadays, I guess this would be called a "pop-up" imprint—the two creators would return to the House of Ideas to recreate *Captain America, Iron Man, Avengers,* and *Fantastic Four* in a separate continuity for 1990s sensibilities. This experiment lasted roughly a year, and featured Jim Lee's re-interpretation of the FF origin, which my pal Michael Bailey (you know him--he's talking Batman elsewhere in this book!) likes to refer to as the FF as rebooted by Michael Bay. In this version, the spaceship *Excelsior* is built by Reed with a revolutionary new "Quantum Drive" designed to take mankind outside our solar system. The ship is financed by Sue and Johnny's organization until it's commandeered by Doctor Doom's forces posing as SHIELD to inspect a stellar anomaly, prompting the four to go up in an earlier prototype to...stop them from using nukes to wipe out the Silver Surfer?

Yeah. The 90's was a powerful drug.

Incidentally, Lee decided to touch on *all* the bases, attributing our heroes' transformation to a combination of cosmic rays, the nuclear detonation, *and* the destruction of the prototype's gamma core. In addition to all this, the four make planetfall in the Caribbean Sea.

It certainly was a different take on the FF (we'll get to another one soon enough), although one that counted as in-continuity; these were the actual FF, not an alternate universe version, but our heroes *stuck* in an alternate universe. As we learn in the back end of the Heroes Reborn run, the four are among a group of heroes and villains whisked away into a pocket universe created by Franklin Richards to prevent their deaths at the hands of Onslaught. For the most part, this pocket universe was soon forgotten save for specific storylines and save for some confusion in following retellings.

Heroes Reborn did not do as well as Marvel hoped it would, which prompted the re-integration of the four titles into the main Marvel Universe under the banner Heroes Return. The following third volume of the *FF* series began with a brief run by Scott Lobdell that led to X-Men Grandmaster Chris Claremont taking the reins. In *FF* v.3 #11 ("The First The Final Fire," 1998), Claremont did his take on the origin story, and as Claremont does, things get... complex. Almost immediately he imposed the possibility of sabotage being a factor in the Fantastic Four's transformation:

"Someone wants this flight stopped! I don't know who, I don't know why, but they've already suborned the other two members of our crew."

"An' there I thought they just up and quit."

The scenario was expanded further, as the spaceship is referred to as "Richard's Folly" due to the mockery of fellow scientists and is designed specifically for four people, thus explaining the presence of Johnny and Sue. The cause of their transformation is walked back to just the cosmic rays and not the mountain of contingencies Jim Lee gave us. On the other hand, Claremont seemed to imply that the quartet hit planetfall on some unspecified island shoreline that could very well be a reference to the Heroes Reborn origin.

The flashbacks to the origin continued in the very next issue (*FF* v.3 #12, "Once More O Green And Pleasant Land," 1998). In that one, Claremont has Johnny go nova right out the box, which prompts Sue to throw up an invisible force field. This is the first time it is implied that Sue had her force field ability from the origin. I suspect this decision was Claremont's way of explaining their development as a kind of "Jean Grey" situation; there is a definite feeling that he was just transferring a lot of his X-Men concepts to the title, and this is no exception.

None of these new facts were followed up on, although I suspect Claremont *really* had a subplot in mind involving the sabotage, and the runs that followed Claremont for a while didn't mess with the origin, except in the case of repositioning the planetfall back to Stockton, California in the first issue of Mark Waid and Mike Wieringo's run (*FF* v3 #60, "Inside Out," 2002), which is also the first issue that coined the term "imaginauts" to describe our heroes.

Now before we move on, we should mention *Ultimate Fantastic Four*, the fifth title in the Ultimate Comics line that was conceived by Bill Jemas, Joe Quesada, Brian Michael Bendis, and Mark Millar. This line was designed to appeal to people who were being drawn into Marvel Comics by the success of the film adaptations. While the Fantastic Four first appeared in issue #9 of *Ultimate Marvel Team-Up*, in a story that was later declared non-canon, their own series began three years later with writer Mark Millar and Adam Kubert behind the wheel. Our four heroes were scaled back to a consistent high-school age and that fateful starship ride was swapped out for an attempt to contact the Negative Zone. This version of the origin would have been considered a curiosity if it wasn't the origin in the ill-fated 2015 FF film.

Going back to the mainstream, Waid's run let the origin stand pat after that, but not so his successor, J. Michael Straczynski. Straczynski, still riding high on his reputation as creator of the *Babylon 5* TV series and the cult comic *Rising Stars*, had established himself at Marvel thanks to newly installed head honchos Bill Jemas and Joe Quesada's love of hiring people from outside comics—something that shot them in the foot more than once (I'm still waiting for Kevin Smith's *Daredevil: Target* #2). Straczynski had been one of their successes thanks to a long and mostly lauded run on Spider Man (we will not talk of Sins Past or One More Day ever again) and was a logical choice on paper to be the next FF scribe.

However, there was Straczynski's tendency to rather cavalierly re-interpret and redefine these characters to contend with. It would end up biting him in the ass sometime later with his runs on *Superman* and *Wonder Woman* over at DC, but at this point the only evidence anyone had of this tendency was the introduction of the "Spider Totem" concept that took up the first few storylines of his Spider-Man run. As such, I don't think anyone was prepared for what he had in store for Marvel's first family.

His first tinkering with the origin was in his second issue (*FF* #528, "Random Factors," 2005). In this story, Reed is working with a group of scientists to recreate the accident that gave the team its powers and is asked to consider something about their origin.

"The consistency and nature of the cosmic rays changed every time they struck one of you. Which is in complete violation of physical law, and it raises a very important question. Why?"

In setting up this concept, Straczynski ignored other incidents where people were exposed to cosmic rays and got different powers (the Red Ghost and his Super-Apes, and old time Hulk enemies the U-Foes), and instead claimed that each member got powers keyed into their personality—Sue, because she was ignored, became invisible; Johnny's emotionality led to him becoming a fire elemental; Ben's belief he had to keep a tough exterior turned him into the Thing; Reed was so stretched thin trying to juggle the different aspects of his life, he became malleable.

This wasn't the first time the idea of the four being shaped by their personality had come up. Roy Thomas explored that idea a number of times in various issues of the first volume of *What If?* but this time it was canon, brought to us by the man who introduced the idea of the "Spider Totem" in *Amazing Spider-Man*, and he wasn't done. With the next issue (*FF* #529, "Appointment Overdue," 2005), Reed has come to the conclusion that their random powers were not an accident, but a byproduct of an attempt by an alien race trying to contact them. Other than some talk about the Voyager, there's no reason Reed makes this connection, or why he felt it was a serious enough matter to sabotage the project. But as we see in issue #530 ("Truth In Flight," 2005) he's right! The team goes into space and actually meets the alien entity that caused the accident, a fellow scientist who, through a telepathic link with the Thing (?), explains that he transcended flesh and blood and was trying to reach out to Reed to begin an exchange of ideas. Oh, and the other beings of his race are trying to track him down for heresy.

And believe or not, that's not all. In issue #531 ("Many Questions, Some Answered"), the entity convinces Reed to allow him to escape into the Negative Zone, bringing the two to…the time before the Big Bang? It is here that the entity reveals that it was his race's desire to understand the "spark of creation" that triggered the creation of the universe.

Ummmm, yeah. According to this version of the origin, Reed Richards and an alien entity made of energy created the universe. And it was that entity, trying to contact Reed so they can do just that, whose actions led to the creation of the FF.

By the time he dropped this bomb, the bloom was off the rose for no-longer-so-young me concerning J. Michael Straczynski and his "redefinition" of the major characters of the Marvel Universe. While I always felt the Fantastic Four needed to be integral to the fabric of Universe 616, I felt this retcon gave them *way* too much credit. I'm not surprised that this new version did not take and has pretty much never been mentioned again.

Thankfully—and I can't believe I'm saying this—Mark Millar came along with the Civil War event to keep Straczynski from taking further steps to cement this reimagining of the origin. It didn't stop him from other ill-advised additions to the lore, though (i.e., the idea that Doctor Doom returns from Hell—Waid left him in Hell—wearing the skin of his childhood friend is a touch…icky). One thing he didn't add to the mythos as much as dusted it off from the periodic attempts to establish it in the 70s and 80s was playing up Reed's arrogance, but then, when your present writer attributes the triggering of the Big Bang and the creation of all life on Earth to you, arrogance is to be accepted.

Dwayne McDuffie, in his attempt at telling the origin in issue #543 ("Com'n Suzie Don't Leave Us Hanging," 2007), was the first to walk back some of the wackier stuff. Back was the hyperspace drive, although the loss-of-government-funding angle introduced by Byrne back in the day was gone. McDuffie doubled down on the "Sue was thirteen, Reed was twenty" awkwardness, sure, but it was actually a pretty fun story at the beginning of what was a pretty great run with an emphasis on character. It is interesting to note that McDuffie did take Straczynski's view on Reed being an arrogant prig and partially readjusted it to make him less monomaniacal while also kind of brushing the whole "he triggered the Big Bang" nonsense under the rug.

(Seriously, people...I don't think people talk as much about the McDuffie run, and in many ways it's as good if not better than some of the runs before and after it. It's fun and much lighter, which was sorely needed after the metaphysical gobbagoo that preceded it.)

You would think the next writer, Jonathan Hickman would make some sweeping changes to the origin. After all, we are talking about the man who plots in terms of years and is not afraid to change *anything* to accommodate his grand vision up to and including destroying whole multiverses. And to be fair, the story he started building toward here didn't get resolved until Hickman finished his subsequent *Avengers* run and the third Secret Wars crossover event. But outside of a strange story that reimagines the origin in Nazi mufti to explain his Interdimensional Council of Reeds (*FF* #605.1, "Origin Story," 2012), Hickman pretty much left well enough alone because, well, he had other things he wanted to redefine at the time.

The first big retcon since MacDuffie was brought to us courtesy then-editor Tom Brevoort himself. In "My Funny Valentine" (*FF* v4 #4, 2013), Matt Fraction adjusted the age of Sue to be in her late teens when she first met Reed. This caused some portions of the audience to protest the decision—yeah, we're coming up on our modern age—which prompted Brevoort to point out in the letters column of *FF* v4 #9 that it was felt that having a thirteen-year-old fall in love with a twenty-year-old was...problematic.

But the biggest retcon—one of the biggest retcons of all—came after a lengthy period where Marvel wasn't even publishing the Fantastic Four. For three years, it was as if the team hadn't existed because Disney was not willing to promote a property whose media rights were at the time owned by 20th Century Fox. The Thing spent time with the Guardians of the Galaxy, the Torch with the Avengers, and the Richards family was nowhere to be seen. Starting with 2017 (and aligning with the start of Disney's campaign to purchase 20th Century outright) and the second volume of *Marvel Two-In-One*, the company began teasing the team, which resulted in the sixth volume of *Fantastic Four* starting in 2018. Chosen to write this next chapter of the team's adventures was Dan Slott.

I should be honest; when it was announced Slott was going to be the new writer, I was quite unimpressed. Slott had done a long run (maybe *too* long) on *Amazing Spider-Man* which saw the character founding his own tech start-up, engaging in a romance with Mockingbird, and participating in the kind of world-trotting shenanigans that didn't make sense for a friendly neighborhood hero. My fear was that Slott was going to do something as out-of-character with Marvel's first family. To my surprise, the things that made me dislike his Spider-Man run are actually the things that make him a great writer for the FF. And it stood to reason he was bound to do his version of the origin...

...which brings us to "Point of Origin," a story that began in issue #14 with the FF's first spacecraft, now called *The Marvel-1*, being put on display in the National Air and Space Museum. In this first sequence Slott started by answering a question that maybe we never asked but should have, depicting in flashback how Johnny Storm went through pilot training under Ben to qualify for the flight, as back-up to the two astronauts originally assigned to the mission who ended up not going. Slott then defined for the first time since Byrne the destination of the craft as well, a binary system forty-four light years away, as well as mentioned a race to develop the first FTL drive. This allowed some of the dialogue in the original Lee/Kirby origin way back in V1 #1 to stand by recontextualizing it in a way that fits into the Sliding Marvel Timeline. We soon learned that Reed had been inspired to rebuild and update the ship as the *Marvel-2* with the intent of finishing the job they started by reaching their destination.

In the following issue, we were introduced to that destination. The world called Spyre is run by a being called the Overseer, protected by a team known as the Unparalleled, and on guard for the arrival of their enemies, "The Four-Told." It seems that Reed's scan for an inhabitable atmosphere was misinterpreted as an attempt to gather intelligence for an invasion. Fearing said invasion, the Overseer creates their own super-team utilizing the same cosmic rays that changed the FF...and also inadvertently a five-hundred-strong monster underclass. Before "Point of Origin" is done, we find out that the cosmic ray storm that assailed the Four all those years ago had been enhanced secretly by the Overseer in the hope that it would kill them before they could authorize this (non-existent) invasion of Spyre. That didn't take, obviously; the four became the Four and you know the rest...except that, to Spyre, they were a long-prophesied threat.

Now, the upshot of Slott's revision and expansion of the origin was that it served as a course-correct for some of the dynamics that had driven a lot of the more recent interpretations of the characters, especially Reed. As he himself spelled out in issue #17:

> *"My shields were strong enough. They always were. We would have landed here unharmed, unchanged. And no possible threat to these people...if not for you, Overseer!"*
>
> *"Reed, you don't mean—"*
>
> *"I do. This man amplified that fateful cosmic storm...he weaponized it and attacked our ship. He created the Fantastic Four!"*

So, yeah—Reed Richards was absolved of the massive hubris of forcing an early launch of his spaceship that led to the creation of the team. This was huge in that it removed what several writers, including Waid and Byrne, claimed to be his motivation. It also made a lot of

133

his callow, dangerous actions reaching all the way back to Gerry Conway having him put his son in a coma to prevent him from developing powers ("The End of The Fantastic Four," 1973) and including the building of a Negative Zone prison during Straczynski's *Civil War*-related issues and getting involved with the Interdimensional Council of Reeds in the Hickman run a little...questionable.

I actually really like it.

Granted, I think this development was done to advance Ben Grimm's character more than Reed's—if there's one complaint I have, it's that the Slott run is far too Thing-centric—but it's a nice fusion of "greatest hits" and new revelations. A number of elements, even outlandish ones like Straczynski's contention that the cosmic storm was controlled by an outside force, were brought together by Slott in a way that makes them into a coherent, even streamlined, whole. It didn't contradict things already established and even found a way to tweak them *just* a bit so that it worked well with that first telling of the origin back in 1961. My only real quibble is with the changing of some of the fiddly bits like the name of the rocket.

As of this writing, Slott has officially ended his tenure and handed writing duties over to David Pepose. While there's no way to know if this writer has plans to alter, retcon, fold, spindle, mutilate, or otherwise change the status quo as set out by his predecessor...but let's be honest. It's bound to happen.

Because of that desire to be part of The World Outside Your Window, the origin of the Fantastic Four demands to be rewritten regularly to keep up with technology, current events, and views of the future. Luckily, we've had some of the best creators alive dealing with the continual need for updating, and while the then-current events Stan and Jack anchored them in was nowhere near as specific as other creations (we're now at a point where Marvel had to create an entire war between two fictitious countries to make Iron Man's origin work), they've provided challenges these creators were more than up to tackling. Even the questionable takes—I'm looking at you, Straczynski—are at least memorable.

Here's hoping the next batch of creators who take the mantle over from Pepose will find new ways to keep the Imaginauts exploring the Fantastic for years to come.

Thomas Deja was born in Brooklyn, NY in 1964. He is a published author of two novels in the Shadow Legion series as well stories in *The Ultimate Hulk*, *X-Men Legends* and *Five Decades of the X-Men*. He is considered one of the first generation of film podcasters thanks to his seven-year collaboration with best friend Derrick Ferguson, *Better In The Dark*, and is still a presence in the podosphere by serving as co-host on *Dread Media*, *The Honeywell Experiment*, and *Not The Loser's Lounge*. Nowadays you can find his serving as Creative Director for 8TW Audio Works, an audio drama collective that produces original and fan adaptations, finally fulfilling a desire he's had ever since picking up a cassette tape of *Abbott and Costello* episodes when he was eleven. Please visit https://8twtheater. blogspot.com/ for further information.

SPIDER-MAN

First Appearance: *Amazing Fantasy* #15, June 5th 1962

The Twisting, Changing Spider-Verse

By Frank Schildiner

In the universe of comic book heroes, there are a few whose origins are so iconic they defy the normal boundaries between fans of the genre and those who find the very concept ludicrous and "childish." It should be noted that many who lived in the latter camp became fans of the Marvel Cinematic Universe film series, but that is an entirely different essay.

Returning to origins, the iconic group that everyone, including my mother whose interest in superheroes somewhere below that of watching paint dry, knows are Superman, Batman, Wonder Woman, and Spider-Man.

It is the last upon this list that we shall consider today and the changes that were made to the history of Peter Parker, the Amazing Spider-Man. Despite my five decades of comic book reading, even I was surprised by the results of my in-depth search into the history of one of the best-known heroes that has ever lived in the minds of millions of fans.

One word of warning; this essay will not cover minor additions to the story of Peter Parker/Spider-Man. For example, in a later story Ben Parker once physically defended his nephew from bullies. While a great memory, it does not really add to the already formidable impact said uncle played in his heroic nephew's life. Also, expansions of villain histories do not really fit what we're doing here. While the shared history of Kraven the Hunter and the Chameleon proved enjoyable and interesting, there is little transformative value beyond providing a reason for their team-ups. We will be focusing on retcons that add greater depths to the already iconic story of Spider-Man himself.

Additionally, over the last decades writers have paid tribute to minor characters whose presence were impactful in the past, but never really expand the origins of Spider-Man. For example, professional wrestler James "Crusher" Hogan once appeared as a janitor in a boxing gym, having spent years telling tales of his supposed friendship with the hero. Spider-Man, out of kindness, confirmed the lies and went about his way. While this, and dozens of other examples, exist over the years, they really don't affect the overall structure of the origin of this legendary superhero. Other than the above example, we'll avoid such stories unless they play a larger part of the overall origin of Spider-Man.

While Spider-Man's earliest appearances on television in the 1967 *Spider-Man* animated series and the PBS *The Electric Company's* Spidey vignettes (1974-1977) did attract many new people to the character, myself included, they didn't change the overall history of the hero. In truth the film that made some impact upon the hero was *Spider-Man* (2002), which granted Peter Parker organic web shooters. This did not go over well with many fans and was dropped after a short time, retconned away by subsequent storylines. Overall, though the above affected the view of Spider-Man, the impact is otherwise minimal.

The classic comic book tale begins simply, one we all know well. Nerdy, bookish, weak, Peter Parker is rejected by his classmates and heads to the science lab. There during an exhibition of radioactivity, a spider is accidentally zapped with the energy on display and bites Parker's hand. He stumbles home, gains the proportionate powers of a spider, and becomes Spider-Man. After the murder of his Uncle Ben, he devotes himself to a selfless battle against evil and becomes a legendary hero.

The famed line, "With great power comes great responsibility" was not actually spoken by Ben Parker in *Amazing Fantasy* #15 (1962) but appeared in a narrative form on the final page. Though said to be spoken by him in subsequent comics, the readers do not actually see Uncle Ben say these famous lines until *Amazing Spider-Man* Vol. 2 #38 (2002). Still, the attribution is otherwise consistent with the storyline from 1963 until the present day.

These facts remain consistent through the many retcons of the Marvel Universe. Even when the truth of radioactivity causing cancer rather than superpowers became known to the public, such details were untouched in the main continuity due to the iconic nature of the hero. Other universes such as that of the Ultimate Spider-Man threw in new ideas which were good, bad, or acceptable. These we will not cover, though I'm still confused by one detail of the Ultimate origin. In that one, the spider had been injected with a prototype of a super-soldier formula. Why would anyone do something so bizarre? Don't they have the *Tarantula!* or *Earth vs. the Spider* films in the Ultimate Universe? Perhaps we should mandate all scientists working with insects spend a period of time watching 1950s sci-fi monster movies as a means of avoiding such insanity.

That aside, Marvel comics kept these essential details intact since the character's first appearance. Whether this was an editorial decision or simply respect for the incredible source material is unknown to me and unimportant in the long run.

Then how can I write an article about the changing origin of Spider-Man if his tale remains the same since he first swung into view in *Amazing Fantasy* #15 (August 1962)? The answer is, everything around Peter Parker's story changed over the years, beginning in areas untouched by the team of Stan Lee and Steve Ditko. Let us begin!

When we meet Peter Parker, he resides with his loving uncle and aunt, Ben and May Parker. We learn his parents are dead in a nebulous, barely discussed "car accident." They endure as just concepts, unimportant figures in our hero's life by the time we arrive in his Queens, New York home. Ben and May are his strong influences, and his parents are just "gone." I will be honest in saying that I don't think I even remembered their names before the Marvel Universe guidebooks listed them in the Spider-Man entry.

This changed for readers in *Amazing Spider-Man Annual* #5 (1968) in a story known as "The Parents of Peter Parker!" While helping Aunt May clean the attic, Peter discovers a trunk filled with pictures and newspaper articles about his parents. In these stories his parents, Richard and Mary Parker, were accused of being Communist agents and traitors to the United States.

Among the shocking items were identification cards for Richard and Mary as members of the Red Skull's organization. This is not the original Red Skull, aka Johann Schmidt, who served as Adolph Hitler's second in command and personal agent of terror. This Red Skull was a Soviet Communist agent named Albert Malik who received the mask and identity of the Skull from Georgy Malenkov (Stalin's successor for two years as Premier of the Soviet Union). He first appeared in *Young Men* #24 (1953), though he was ultimately pushed aside once the original, Nazi version of the masked monster returned to the pages of Marvel Comics.

With the aid of the Fantastic Four, Peter Parker pursues the Malik Red Skull and defeats his organization. It was then that he discovers Richard and Mary Parker were, in fact, C.I.A. infiltration operatives working for the United States. Their murder was carried out by his top assassin, Karl Fiers, aka "The Finisher," who also was allegedly the personal trainer of Dmitri Smerdyakov, aka the supervillain known as "The Chameleon." The connection between the Finisher and the Chameleon was a later day addition to the history of the Spider-verse, having first emerged in *Giant-Size Amazing Spider-Man: Chameleon Conspiracy* #1 (2021).

Years later, the Parkers return in the form of Life Model Decoys (LMD), with the Richard robot possessing the harsh, unpleasant attitudes of his creator/programmers, Chameleon and Harry Osborn. Peter Parker has a breakdown when he discovers this was a ruse, though some healing came when the LMD Mary Parker goes against orders and saves his life.

The death of the Parkers was alleged to have been a plane crash, but in Peter's mind, they were cleared of wrongdoing. What he did not discover at that time was that his parents may have had another child, a daughter born shortly before their murder at the hands of the Finisher. Allegedly their second child, Theresa Elizabeth Parker, was born in secret and adopted by an unknown family. Her first appearance was in *Amazing Spider-Man: Family Business* #1 (2014).

We readers learn that Theresa Parker followed her parents in the intelligence world, becoming a covert C.I.A. agent who was battling the Kingpin and his criminals. They traveled together to Cairo, Egypt where they prevented Wilson Fisk's attempt at claiming a Sleeper robot as well as the dangerous powers of the mutant telepath, Mentallo. Theresa's actual familial connection to Peter Parker is purposefully left nebulous and it's unknown if they are brother/sister or if she is an unknowing infiltration agent trained by the Finisher and Chameleon.

It is highly unlikely we'll ever receive a definite answer, but that's just fine. The idea that Spider-Man's origins do not begin in a small home in Queens, New York is acceptable to some readers, rejected by others.

Personally, I'm not a fan of the James Bond-styled additions to Peter Parker's lineage. The character has always been, at least in my view, a positive and truthful view of a highly intelligent person with issues closer to that of the common man. While Spider-Man may exist as a magnificent hero who accomplishes incredible feats, Peter Parker's life is difficult and troubled. He struggles with the rent, struggles for a time with even getting a date, as well as bullies and inner guilt based on his past. Adding the idea that his parents were accomplished secret agents lessens that to some extent. The Ultimate comics had Richard Parker as an engineer, which seems more fitting, at least based on the original origin. Still, the secret agent bit has become canon and does impact the greater origin.

Returning to Peter Parker's earliest moments before turning into Spider-Man, we meet other characters who did not appear at the time of the original series but were injected into his origin.

The first is a bully Peter experienced throughout childhood by the name of Carl King. While everyone knows Flash Thompson was an unpleasant character who later became more cartoonish in his behavior, Carl King was the more traditional bully. He was large, unpleasant looking, issued threats, and demanded Peter's lunch money. When he couldn't comply, Carl would lift him bodily and jam the pre-Spider-Man Peter into a school toilet.

As it happens, Carl King was present when the radioactive spider bit Peter Parker and witnessed the subsequent display of newly gained superpowers. As such, wishing to have such abilities, he broke into the laboratory and stole the dead spider. Not being high on the intelligence scale, Carl King ate the dead radioactive spider in hopes of repeating the experiment. This is an original, if completely bizarre and disgusting, method for gaining powers.

Carl King did succeed in one way: the radioactive spider he munched on did exude enough transformative effects to grant him abilities unimagined by all but the most diseased imaginations. Unfortunately for the former bully, the powers gained were horrific in the extreme.

The body of Carl King transforms into a mass of several thousand spiders, all of whom possess his mind as part of some nightmarish collective intelligence. He then discovers that if he ate a victim from within, he could wear the unfortunate person's skin. Calling himself the Thousand, Carl King murders J. Jonah Jameson's secretary, Jess Patton, with the idea of stealing Peter Parker's skin and identity. His plans do not work out and in the end his collective arachnid body appears reduced to a single spider form. This fleeing spider dies under the foot of a New York pedestrian, possibly destroying Peter Parker's former bully forever. A unique, if horrifying, addition to the origin of Spider-Man. This was one I really liked since it adds a degree of cosmic horror to Spider-Man that I hadn't foreseen.

Remaining for a little longer at the radioactive lab, our energy ladened arachnid has not completed his painful spreading of superpowers quite yet. Prior to Carl King consuming the dead spider, said beastie bites one other person. Just after Peter Parker receives his bite, the spider crawls across the room and bites a woman named Cindy Moon on the ankle. This occurs in *Amazing Spider-Man* Vol. 3 #1 (2014).

Cindy Moon is a highly intelligent student whose mother insists she attend the field trip to the lab. There, after being bitten by the spider, she receives a lesser dose of the DNA-changing irradiated venom. Unlike Peter Parker, she gains the ability to create biological spider webbing, which traps her unfortunate parents. An elderly man named Ezekiel Sims comes for her, revealing he too possesses arachnid-based powers. He trains her in their powers, having knowledge of methods of fighting as well as the finer use of these skills.

Ezekiel Sims apparently derives his power through totemic magic which he uses as a means of making a fortune. What the readers also later find out is that this elder spider-dude also comes with a dimension-hopping supervillain named Morlun. Morlun, who resembles a freaky mixture of Dracula, Morbius the Living Vampire, and an emo with better than usual fashion sense, is a totem hunter. He travels to different worlds hunting spider totem beings and absorbs their energy.

Managing to get away from this enemy, Ezekiel Sims constructs a special room in his tower that blocks the energy vampire's tracking powers. For thirteen years Cindy Moon remains in protective custody until Spider-Man discovers her existence through the Watcher's orb. She warns him about the energy vampire, but Peter frees her anyway, having already defeated Morlun in a brutal series of battles.

Taking the codename Silk, Cindy Moon joins Peter Parker battling supervillains such as the Black Cat and Electro before heading off as a hero who works with other dimension hopping/time jumping spider-heroes. Silk, who briefly uses the codename Silkworm for unfathomable reasons, still exists at Marvel as a hero who occasionally works with Spider-Man facing menaces such as the Goblin Nation and the Sin Eater.

As for Morlun, he dies twice by the hands of Spider-Man, once because of the radioactivity in Peter's blood, the other time because his powers mutate Spider-Man into a hideous spider creature with arm stingers and vicious, sharp fangs. He later returns, hunting the Black Panther as well as going another round with Spider-Man.

Oh, and we're not done yet with the old radioactive lab quite yet. Remember that spider who bit two people and got eaten by a very deranged bully? Well, apparently it didn't quite die but split into two spiders. One dies and becomes Carl King's deranged snack while the other similarly transforms. This spider receives the intelligence of a human as well as the ability to speak as seen in *Marvel's Voices* Vol. 1 #1 (2020).

Called "Goddess" by a scientist who speaks to her, this arachnid becomes a Gamma-mutate like the Incredible Hulk, the Leader, the Abomination, and other beings similarly transformed. In addition to gaining an impressive intellect and, somehow, the ability to speak, Goddess can grow her body to massive size, becoming every spider-based sci-fi nightmare I had as a child in one comic character. While still possessing the primal urges of a spider and the need for meat, Goddess is something of a heroic figure who views Spider-Man and Silk as her extended family. Though I found the concept completely frightening, I can't hate a spider who enjoys reading one of my favorite novels, *The Three Musketeers*.

These tales are a massive transformation within the mythology relating to Spider-Man. Let's start with the fact that the radioactive spider that changed nebbish Peter Parker into one of the most important superheroes in comics has, over the last fifty or so years, become a semi-heroic being who views him as its family. Add to that the idea that two more characters were affected by the creature, the heroic Cindy Moon, and a repugnant Carl King, and Spider-Man's origins have expanded in unexpected directions. One little zapped spider impacted many lives in ways unheard of in comics.

However, these changes and transformations pale when compared to the overall effect of Morlun and Ezekiel Sims. The idea that Spider-Man is not a unique concept is stunning, that there are possibly infinite numbers of such beings both expands and lessens the influence of the character of this hero. Yes, we already knew and acknowledged some other worlds possess a Peter Parker/Spider-Man. Whether they were the Ultimate-verse or the many created in the often wonderful "What if…?" series, Morlun's origin enlarges this conceptual basis into a mystical direction untouched by previous continuity.

Morlun and Ezekiel Sims are based in a totemic view of heroism, with the latter receiving his powers through ceremonial magic rather than weird science. This is a two-sided coin that could be effective for the long-term series but appears in conflict with the established history. T'Challa, aka the Black Panther, received his powers through totemic magic and an herbal infusion. Peter Parker/ Spider-Man received his DNA-altering powers through the impact of uncontrolled science in conflict with basic humanity. I cannot say whether this addition to the origin tale is a good one, merely that it adds layers that were probably undreamed of at the time Lee and Ditko crafted the original tale.

One of the most important figures in the Spider-Man universe is, without question, Mary Jane Watson (Parker). Her name floated about for some time in the comics, with Aunt May and Mary Jane's Aunt Anna attempting to set them up for some time. We eventually meet her in one of the most legendary introductions and the renowned line, "Face it, Tiger…you just hit the jackpot!" Mary Jane was the top rival for Peter's affections against the gentle Gwen Stacy. Readers preferred the extroverted, carefree, red-headed, party girl to her kindly blond opposite. Their relationship had many ups and downs, but otherwise followed continuity until *Amazing Spider-Man* Vol.1 #257 (1984). That was the day Mary Jane Watson revealed she had known Peter Parker was Spider-Man for some time but had kept the secret to herself.

There are several versions of how she figured this startling information, but most hold that it was on the same night Ben Parker died. This added a great deal of depth to her character as well as again changing the original origin. In the past, very few people knew the truth of the Peter Parker/Spider-Man connection. Placing this in the hands of Mary Jane, retroactively since Day One, changes the history in many important ways. The biggest part is that all subsequent stories, until the unfortunate 2007-08 "One More Day" storyline, held the twist that Spider-Man always had one person supporting him in his endeavors. Later two other former love interests joined these ranks in the form of Carlie Cooper and Felicia Hardy, aka the Black Cat, though their overall effect on the Spider-universe history is limited.

One of the earliest moments of Peter Parker's origins, before he became Spider-Man, was a series of panels in which he was both disregarded and bullied by his fellow teens at Midtown High. We view our poor hero as he asks a girl named Sally out on a date, only to have her reject him in favor of a "dreamboat" named Flash Thompson.

Marvel history left her behind, with Liz Allen occupying her place until we discovered an important facet of Spider-Man's history. Events surrounding Sally, who we later learn possessed the surname of Avril, one whose brief connection to Peter Parker as Spider-Man, had an obvious effect upon his psyche forward.

In *Untold Tales of Spider-Man* Vol.1 #10-13 (1996) we meet Sally once again and discover that she and her boyfriend, Jason Ionello, are fans of the idea of Spider-Man. She discovers that Peter is the photographer who has specialized in producing photographs of their hero and attempts to blackmail him with the knowledge of his position. Oh, and she's dressed in a blond wig and a costume, calling herself Bluebird, and wants him to take her picture. Sally seems to see superheroing as a chance for fame, which Peter rejects due to the danger that world holds.

The next day Peter reveals his job as a photographer to his classmates, receiving false adulation from Flash Thompson and annoyance from the blackmailing Sally Avril. Later, in costume, he tells her that she should abandon her ambitions since the world she's trying to enter is deadly. This is proven correct when her attempts at helping Spider-Man in a battle against Electro and Eel were useless. In fact, her actions allow them to escape. After several escapades where Bluebird endangers Spider-Man's efforts, he finally looks the other way when she's punched in the stomach by a criminal.

Sally Avril retires as Bluebird, coming up with the notion of becoming a crime photographer and eclipsing Peter Parker at the Bugle. Discovering that the villain version of Black Knight and his crew were holding an archduke hostage, Sally and Jason rush to the scene in his convertible. Spider-Man was battling the Black Knight at the time but witnessed the duo run a red light. Their car was struck broadside and Sally died after being thrown from the car.

Spider-Man discussed this with an unseen hero the readers later found out was his friend the Human Torch. He blamed himself for Sally's death, believing if he had let her remain as Bluebird, perhaps she wouldn't have died so tragically. Johnny Storm rejects this guilt, stating that Sally could have died at the hands of the Black Knight or any number of criminals they face regularly. Still, Peter Parker feels guilty despite receiving reassurance from his friend about his heroic actions protecting the archduke and that man's daughter.

This early addition to the origin and history of Spider-Man demonstrates an additional layer of guilt as well as a reason for his continuing actions as a hero. Unlike Sally Avril, who Peter Parker liked and admired to a degree, his actions as Spider-Man are based on the right choice. The guilt of Uncle Ben's and Sally Avril's deaths remains with him, as is the realization that he took up his cause for selfless reasons. His early brushes with fame aside, Peter Parker's calling as Spider-Man is for the right reasons. Though this often complicated his life in his post high school years, there was no question that he could easily leave the mantle of Spider-Man behind. Oh, and Sally later resurfaced as a clone who may have survived another of Miles Warren's bizarre experiments, so she may one day return and learn of Peter Parker's guilt over her death.

One iconic moment that altered the Spider-Man universe could have been a minor one were it not for the genius of the amazing Stan Lee and the equally incredible Steve Ditko. They created a storyline known as "If This Be My Destiny...!" in *The Amazing Spider-Man* Vol.1 #31–33 (1965-1966) which has become one of the most celebrated arcs in comics history, let alone the Spider-Man series.

Spider-Man battles Doctor Octopus, who had been using the identity of the Master Planner to steal technology as well as a rare isotope capable of saving May Parker's life. Octopus, at his most diabolical, leaves Spider-Man trapped under an enormous pile of metal equipment that was slowly crushing him to death. Over the course of five pages, with unrivaled art by Ditko, Peter Parker re-members the reason for his fight as Spider-Man as well as the love he receives from his friends and family. Every word in this sequence appeared filled with an almost Shakespearian power, raising the en-tire artform of comics to the level of that of great literature. To this day, this sequence is one of the most beloved and copied ideas in the world of comics.

Though the creators of Spider-Man and other amazing charac-ters, Stan Lee and Steve Ditko managed in five pages to change Spider-Man forever. The character was no longer merely a wise-cracking, fun-loving, teen hero, but one with powerful motivations and a desire to protect those he holds dear. Battling against odds far beyond his apparent limitations, "If This Be My Destiny...!" dem-onstrated that Peter Parker's Spider-Man was capable of depths far beyond his original creation. Additionally, the art is still unmatched and has become one of the gold standards in the industry. I often wonder if this five-page sequence is the reason Spider-Man is one of the flagship characters of Marvel Comics. I still remember the first time I read the story and recall holding my breath and almost shak-ing as I wondered how Peter Parker would survive such a terrible trap. This pleasurable experience is what makes good comics rise to the status of legendary.

Final note: to this day this sequence and storyline consistently rank among the top twenty greatest in Marvel history. This is a heri-tage that clearly demonstrates the place these five pages hold in the minds of comic fans, many of whom rarely consider the older books worthy of note.

An impressive transformation and addition to the Spider-verse occurred in the early 1980's during the tenure of Roger Stern and John Romita Jr. as writer and artist, respectively, upon the series. According to Stern, fans of the series sought the return of the Green Goblin as a major villain of the series. This was a time when major character deaths remained unchanged and neither writer nor artist sought the return of the latter-day Goblins.

This began a slow storyline in the series beginning in *Amazing*

Spider-Man Vol. 1 #238 (1983), in which an unknown figure sought the devices and notes of the original Green Goblin. The notes for the Goblin formula were analyzed and improved, and the shadowy person bathed in the chemicals rather than having them explode in his face like his predecessor. According to Roger Stern, the idea was to hide the identity of the future Hobgoblin for one issue longer than was used for the Norman Osborn Green Goblin. The look of the Hobgoblin, though based on the Green Goblin, was originally created by John Romita Jr. Additionally, they had no original plan for the actual identity, with Stern deciding on the wealthy Roderick Kingsley early in the process.

As to the identity, there were also suggestions that Kingsley had a twin brother Daniel who also took the Hobgoblin role, but this plan was mooted as a bad idea with little setup. After Roger Stern left the title, Tom DeFalco took over and believed the actual identity was that of the Kingpin's son, Richard Fisk. DeFalco apparently was having difficulties with editor Jim Owsley over this subject and lied, stating the Hobgoblin was actually Ned Leeds. Leeds was later murdered by the Foreigner while dressed in the Hobgoblin identity and the former Jack O'Lantern merc, Jason Macendale, took his place until merged with a demon to become Demogoblin.

Roger Stern, unhappy with these events, revealed in 1997 that Roderick Kingsley was always the Hobgoblin, and that Ned Leeds was a hypnotized fall guy. Murdering the demon purged Macendale, and he took back his identity to remain as the Hobgoblin since that time. His identity was fully accepted after being unmasked in *Spider-Man: Hobgoblin Lives* #3 (1997). Though briefly replaced by Phil Urich in the identity, Kingsley has been one of Spider-Man's most dangerous foes since the start.

Hobgoblin appears to have been a major bridge for the series between the old and new periods of the character. The Spider-Man saga has always been a demonstration of the changes one can undergo in life, with Peter Parker progressing through his story as an impressive superhero and a man whose personal life was never ideal. The difficulty lay often in the nostalgia of past events preventing the creation of new challenges. By the 1980s the need for new enemies was growing, though readers still desired the pleasure of the classic villains.

Roger Stern and John Romita Jr. cleverly created a new supervillain who acknowledged the genius of the original ideas while breaking new grounds. The Hobgoblin proved an effective menace for Spider-Man, even going so far as attempting to become a major crime boss in concert with Richard Fisk also-known-as The Rose. With this successful addition to the series, writers began taking greater chances and creating new dangers for the hero. I am not sure, without the presence of the Hobgoblin, whether writers would have attempted some of their wilder storylines which have occurred since that time. I for one am grateful to both men, even if subsequent writers were somewhat clunky in their usage of the Hobgoblin and other enemies.

Though a backup story in *Amazing Spider-Man* Vol.1 #248 (1984), the Roger Stern tale, "The Kid Who Collects Spider-Man," ranks among the most moving comic stories in the history of the genre, in which Spider-Man visits a boy named Timothy "Tim" Harrison. Tim collects items from Spider-Man's career, including reels of his early television appearances, bullets from cases, newspaper and magazine articles, and so many other items. Spider-Man spends hours with him, touched by the child's devotion to his heroic careers.

Before leaving, Tim asks Spider-Man his real identity. After a moment's hesitation, the hero removes his mask and reveals his secret. He also tells of his actions in the early days as well as the death of Uncle Ben. Tim remains Spider-Man's greatest fan despite the sad story and the two embrace before Peter Parker leaves. It is then revealed that Tim Harrison is in a cancer ward, dying from leukemia. A newspaper article had been written about his dying wish, to meet his hero Spider-Man before passing away. Peter Parker weeps for the young man, his greatest fan and a gentle, kind child as the story ends.

No battles, no action, no sexy shots of nurses, or any of the other tactics used in the promotion of comic sales. This was a human-interest tale along the lines of a Will Eisner comic, which was the intention of Roger Stern from the start. He stated in a 1996 interview, "Partly, I'm sure that it sprang from a desire on my part to do a short human-interest story in the style of Will Eisner—that's why the story is partially advanced through newspaper clippings...I was trying to be Eisneresque."

In my lengthy years as a fan of comics and the universes of these characters, I have only twice been moved to tears by the work of stories. Coincidentally, both occurred in 1984, with the other being "Who is Donna Troy" in *New Teen Titans* Vol.1 issue #38 (1984). Stern's story in particular was a truly incredible addition to the Spider-verse, providing a different view of the Marvel Universe as well as one of their prime heroes. It is easy to get lost in battles, conspiracies, soap opera type tales, and the history of a hero such as Spider-Man.

What Roger Stern managed to do in a few short pages is to expand the Marvel Universe to the microlevel. Tim Harrison is a regular person, more like you or I, than his hero. In this story Tim battles a foe that we ourselves face daily, an enemy of life that renders a superhero like Spider-Man helpless...cancer. Many of us, myself included, have lost family and loved ones to this disease and the pain Peter Parker feels upon leaving the bedside of his greatest fan is real and familiar. There were no saccharine solutions to Timothy Harrison's forthcoming death, only the pain and sadness his passing will bring to any who know him. Roger Stern, for a brief time, made each reader connect to the Peter Parker Spider-Man on a human level. As we read those pages, the helplessness cancer brings touched millions of readers and remains one of the most important stories in the lengthy history of this amazing hero.

As I said, I cried after I read that story and became a greater fan of the character. Because in a brief tale, he became as helpless as me and suffering in a way I understood. Few stories can say that had such an important effect upon a superhero as "The Kid Who Collects Spider-Man."

In the lengthy history of Marvel Comics, there are many storylines of note. Spider-Man has been part of a fair number of these sequences and will no doubt continue to do so in the future. One standout storyline that impressed even non-fans of the Peter Parker series is that of "Fearful Symmetry: Kraven's Last Hunt" or simply, "Kraven's Last Hunt."

Kraven the Hunter, aka Sergei Kravinoff, has been a part of the Spider-verse since *Amazing Spider-Man* Vol.1 issue #15 (1964). A Russian immigrant whose family were nobles, he was a legendary big game hunter who viewed Spider-Man as a challenge worthy of his skills. He fails, joins the Sinister Six, fails again there, battles Ka-Zar and eventually is relegated to the position of that of a lesser legacy villain.

Enter writer J. M. DeMatteis, who had this storyline idea in the past but never executed it prior to 1987. Running through *Web of Spider-Man* Vol.1 #31–32, *Amazing Spider-Man* Vol.1 #293–294, and *Peter Parker, the Spectacular Spider-Man* Vol.1 #131–132 from October-November 1987, the storyline was magnificent, transformative, and written in a way that has been the source of imitations since that time.

Kraven, recognizing his failures in life, reaches his full potential while considering his battles with Spider-Man. He attacks Spider-Man and guns his enemy down, apparently killing Peter Parker. Donning Spider-Man's black costume, he briefly becomes the "hero" and defeats street criminals before Mary-Jane Parker realizes this is not her husband since his actions lack the inner decency apparent even when he battles foes.

As a final challenge to his new role, Kraven battles the creature known as Vermin, a genetically modified monster which Spider-Man previously required the aid of Captain America to defeat. Unlike his seemingly dead foe, Kraven subdues Vermin single-handedly, proving to himself that he was always greater than Spider-Man.

Meanwhile, Spider-Man awakens in a coffin buried alive. He was, in fact, drugged by Kraven and left six feet under. Reuniting with his wife, he tracks down Kraven, who gives him the choice of recapturing the newly released Vermin or beating Sergei Kravinoff who would not fight back. Ever the hero, Peter Parker chases down and captures the monster as Kraven returns home, having completed his last hunt. He then kills himself and remains dead in Marvel comics until 2009.

Kraven's Last Hunt is a work of art, a Spider-verse story from the point-of-view of the villain. Kraven was often seen as a joke character, a useless enemy who could never be a true menace to Spider-Man without assistance from more successful villains like Doctor Octopus. J. M. DeMatteis held these views but rose above them and raised Kraven the Hunter to the status of legendary foe through this story arc.

One of the greatest moments occurs when Spider-Man, catching up with Kraven, punches the man who "killed" him and stole his identity. Sergei Kravinoff does not fight back, instead, with blood on his lips, he smiles and welcomes the attack. He explains to Peter Parker that he will not battle him because he already won. This was his last hunt, proving to himself that he, Sergei Kravinoff, is the better man in their war.

Whew, this one still ranks as of my favorite comic arcs since I read it during the first run. Kraven's Last Hunt was like reading a Russian novel rather than a comic book. Kraven the Hunter's status as a ridiculous villain irrevocably ended during this storyline and Peter Parker was forced to reassess his entire existence. DeMatteis's work demonstrated that even weak, ridiculous villains can be amazing if used properly. Additionally, Spider-Man was never quite the same again, with his adventures taken on a darker tone as fit this arc as well as the trend of the period.

One of the most impressive and Marvel Universe-affecting retcons was the return of the legendary supervillain Norman Osborn aka the Green Goblin. His death by being impaled by his own Goblin Glider was one of the important events in the history of Spider-Man, with others trying to step up and take his place as the literal archnemesis of Peter Parker/Spider-Man. Though some, such as Hobgoblin, came close, no one character possessed the sheer fiendish menace as the late Norman Osborn.

This changed in *Peter Parker Spider-Man* Vol.1 #75 (1996) when Norman returns. We discover he never actually died but was in a coma and had his body replaced with that of a homeless man. He returns, as vicious and as brilliant as ever, with a desire for revenge.

According to later stories, many of Spider-Man's problems since the false death were manipulations by Norman—Miles Warren and his clone crisis was just one of the many terrible schemes orchestrated by this evil puppet-master.

This return was hailed by most as a brilliant move and latter-day tales prove this retcon was a clever idea. Norman Osborn is considered one of the most important supervillains in the entirety of the Marvel Universe, having affected every superhero in one way or another. He even rose to become the head of United States secret intelligence, having replaced S.H.I.E.L.D. with S.W.O.R.D. and taken the director's seat. Additionally, during the period, he led the Avengers, better known as the Dark Avengers, and acted as a combination of Captain America and Iron Man in the armor of the Iron Patriot. While not all retcons to the history of Spider-Man are well-received, this one appears to have been a success beyond the dreams of the writers and editors.

The downside of the return of Norman Osborn comes down to the Marvel writer's need to put their stamp upon this character, the universe's top villain. In the last few years Norman lost his powers thanks to the actions of the Superior Spider-Man, wore a castoff Iron Man suit as the Iron Patriot, gained the powers of the Super-Adaptoid, merged with the Carnage symbiote to become the Red Goblin, and finally regained his Green Goblin powers. To say this is a bit much is putting it mildly, and many fans, based on my readings over the years, roll their eyes at the latest iteration of Norman Osborn's abilities. Just my opinion, but the editors at Marvel need to place a moratorium on writer's transforming this character into their pet monster.

Since I cited Miles Warren earlier, now is as good a time as any to discuss his massive impact upon the history of Spider-Man. Briefly summarizing his motivations, Miles Warren was a biochemistry professor at Empire State University, first appearing in *Amazing Spider-Man* Vol.1 #31 (1965). We later find out he was much, much more than that, having served as a lab assistant to none other than the High Evolutionary. This basically means he was trained in genetics by a being whose power level is close to that of Galactus (under certain writers).

According to later lore, Warren successfully created the High Evolutionary's New Men, his Dr. Moreau-inspired combination of man and beast. One of Miles Warren's successes was a merger of his own DNA with that of a jackal. This being later murdered Warren's wife and child, so I guess we can call this a qualified success.

In the end, said Evolutionary expelled Miles Warren for being too good at his job as well as giving the New Men a charismatic leader. That sounds a bit suspect but moving on. Miles Warren was Peter Parker's teacher and fell madly in love with Gwen Stacy...as everyone seemed to do in comics. When she died, his mental status, which appeared shaky at best, shattered and he went insane. Thus begins the first Clone Saga, a series of events whose addition to the Spider-Man universe is still felt today.

Discovering that his lab partner, Anthony Serba, who looked a lot like Peter Lorre in my opinion, successfully cloned a frog, Professor Miles Warren gave the man some human tissue in *Amazing Spider-Man* Vol.1 #149 (1975). Serba soon discovered this was human tissue and objected over humanitarian reasons. Warren murdered him and the act caused a new identity to appear in his mind, that of the Jackal.

As we all know, the Jackal created his own Gwen Stacy and later a new Peter Parker/Spider-Man. Through a series of events that are long, convoluted, and involve battles with the Scorpion and the Tarantula, an attempted murder of Spider-Man on the Brooklyn Bridge in an attempt at recreating Gwen Stacy's death, and the destruction of New York's Shea Stadium, Peter Parker faced off with his clone to fight him. Parker won, the clone died, and he disposed of it by dropping the body into a smokestack/incinerator in *Amazing Spider-Man* Vol 1 #149 (1975).

Now, one would think this would be the end of the tale, but as all Spider-Man readers know, nothing could be further from the truth. Let's break down some of the major events that followed. The Gwen Stacy clone existed until *Spectacular Spider-Man Annual*

Vol 1 #8 (1988). Then it is revealed she never was a clone, but a woman named Joyce Delaney who was infected with a virus that transformed her into a duplicate of Gwen Stacy. By the same token, the Spider-Man clone was apparently Anthony Serba who was infected with a Peter Parker virus.

Unfortunately, the above story also turned out to be a lie. Joyce Delaney was a Gwen clone, the Spider-Man clone wasn't Serba, and somehow Miles Warren substituted a dead clone of Peter Parker for the real one in *Scarlet Spider Unlimited* Vol 1 #1 (1995). Yes, very, very confusing, but I have a real reason for discussing this long, overly convoluted tale: Simply put, the return of the clone of Peter Parker.

The clone, who calls himself Ben Reilly, returns to the world in *Spectacular Spider-Man* Vol 1 #216 (1994), having left town after the Clone Saga and returning upon hearing of Aunt May's illness. Throughout the storyline, known as "The Exile Returns," Ben claims he is the real Peter Parker and the one currently married and living in Manhattan is the clone. He adopts the superhero codename of the Scarlet Spider, and the "real" Spider-Man retires.

Originally, this was intended to be the end of the storyline, with Peter Parker taking a break and Ben Reilly becoming Spider-Man. However, the powers that be at Marvel changed their minds and it was revealed that Ben was the clone, and the idea that he was the real Peter Parker was a fabrication of Norman Osborn. Then, Ben Reilly died again. But wait! He later returns, becomes the new Jackal, becomes a hero again, and is apparently working with the clone of Jean Grey aka the Goblin Queen these days. Oh, and there is another, messed up clone known as Kaine out there too, but let's not dive down that rabbit hole.

If you are confused by the twists and turns, don't feel bad. Everyone found all of the above very hard to follow and the ideas were universally panned by readers and critics. However, feelings aside, few stories ever affected a character as massively as the Clone Sagas did with the character of Spider-Man. To this day there is debate as to whether Peter Parker or Ben Reilly is the original or if even both might be clones. I can tell you that I tried simplifying the maze of stories and retcons but have little doubt there are dozens of minor changes only the most devoted fan could remember.

Just as a side note, the Ultimate Universe also had a Clone Saga, but it was far, far simpler. In that one we meet Spider-Woman/Jessica Drew who is a female clone of Peter Parker. There are twisted clones too, but many of the mind-bending, confusing concepts are part of the main continuity. A rare moment in which the alternate universe did a better job with the same idea.

On a more positive note, one history changing move occurred when Spider-Man debuted his symbiotic costume in *Amazing Spider-Man* Vol 1 #252 (1984). The all-black costume interested readers and proved a positive idea for a time. Later, we discovered that he received the symbiotic alien during the Secret Wars event, which occurred prior to the debut, in *Marvel Superheroes Secret Wars* Vol 1 #8 (1984).

The alien proved dangerous, and Spider-Man rid himself of it through the use of sonics in the form of church bells. Four years later the symbiote returned with a new host named Eddie Brock, a disgraced journalist who blamed Spider-Man for his career failures. Praying at the church where Spider-Man expelled the alien, the symbiote dropped on him and they merged, forming Venom. Venom had all of Spider-Man's powers, greater strength because Eddie Brock was a powerful man physically, and he knew Peter Parker's secret identity.

Thus began a period where the character of Venom appeared just about everywhere in Spider-Man comics. Soon the villain was considered as dangerous as the Green Goblin and Doctor Octopus, and the bizarre character became incredibly popular and influenced a host of changes throughout the Marvel Universe. After a time, Venom became more of an antihero, with fellow symbiotes Carnage, Scream, Lasher, Phage, Agony, Riot, Hybrid, Toxin, Mania, Scorn, and Sleeper following. Eddie Brock, thanks to having his cancer cured by Mister Negative's powers, even ends up inadvertently creating another symbiote named Anti-Venom that fought others of this alien race.

Since that time, Eddie Brock has gained and lost Venom several times, with the creature at one time taking over Mac Gargan, aka the Scorpion, and serving as Spider-Man on the Dark Avengers with Norman Osborn's Iron Patriot. These aliens now possess a backstory nearly as complex as other famed Marvel aliens such as the Skrulls and Kree, though are more commonly in the spotlight. Few concepts in comics grow as exponentially as that of these symbiotes, known as "Klyntar," taking on a life of their own.

From a simple costume to an entire race of beings influenced by Peter Parker, the symbiote has become synonymous with the Spider-Man universe. Since the creation and many subsequent appearances in comics, cartoons, and video games, Venom has fostered three movie appearances, in *Spider-Man 3* (2007), *Venom* (2018), and *Venom: Let There Be Carnage* (2021). The character has transformed Spider-Man's universe in unexpected and often enjoyable ways that have made him one of the most important in the comics world.

There were many controversial Spider-Man stories over the years, some of which are legends in the minds of readers for their poor reception. The two Clone Sagas cover this area and may have had some origin impact had the resolutions not been a precise return to status quo. However, every single one of the Spider-Man storylines from start to present day pale in comparison to the grotesque, retcon inducing, storyline known as "Sins Past" in *Amazing Spider-Man* Vol.1 #509-514 (2004).

In this story, Peter Parker meets a woman with a remarkable resemblance to Gwen Stacy. Her name is Sarah Stacy, and she claims that she and her brother Gabriel are the children of Gwen and Peter. They were raised in France by Norman Osborn and aged rapidly due to the unstable elements in their blood due to their father's altered DNA.

This was bad enough, but Marvel had barely scratched the surface. The above was a lie, Sarah and Gabriel were the children of Gwen Stacy...and Norman Osborn. To make matters worse, Mary Jane claims she knew of this, having overheard a discussion between the pair on the subject. Peter accepts this as true and immediately concludes that Gwen Stacy's death in *Amazing Spider-Man* Vol. 1 #121 (1973) was an intentional murder out of jealousy. Comic history's most famous death was now a near-illegal love triangle unworthy of a 90's nighttime soap opera.

Whew, just writing that one paragraph summary made me feel I need a long shower, preferably in ammonia. To call this storyline terrible is an insult to poor writing, the implications in a larger sense as wrongheaded as that of *Avengers* Vol.1 #200 (1980). If you don't know that one, read up on it; it's legendary in its misogynistic details.

To call this Gwen tale a major change to Spider-Man's backstory is too light a statement. This was a universe-shattering concept, one whose implications spread exponentially through the entirety of the Marvel Universe. The idea that the forty-something supervillain Norman Osborn not only had an affair with a teen Gwen Stacy transformed the history of the Peter Parker character from his college years straight up to and including the "One More Day" storyline that reset his entire continuity and removed the Peter/MJ marriage.

This storyline caused a massive backlash from fans of the series as well as professionals in the business. The writer/creator of the concept wanted Sarah and Gabriel Stacy to be the children of Peter Parker and Gwen Stacy, but Marvel's editors vetoed the ideas as aging the character too much in the long term. Instead, they created this misogynistic secondary plan and appeared surprised by the subsequent fan reaction. Gwen Stacy was written as a paragon of virtue and while that made her less interesting than the depth of Mary Jane Watson, it was a memory that this tainted deeply. Also, the overt implications of the implied relationship were simply grotesque and inappropriate.

Regardless of fandom's feelings, this remained canon through several universe reboots, finally receiving a soft reboot that removed the repulsive portions of the storyline. In the "Sinister War" storyline from *Amazing Spider-Man* Vol.5 #70-73 (2021), writer Nick Spencer transformed the storyline into something that, while not good, was at least not completely horrific.

We discover that Harry Osborn, during his time as the Green

Goblin, was behind this entire false tale. Apparently, Norman Osborn sold a young Harry's soul to Mephisto in return for wealth and success. Discovering this, Harry, who was insane from the Goblin formula, enlists the aid of Norman's former partner Mendel Stromm to genetically engineer two children from Norman and Gwen Stacy's DNA who he named Gabriel and Sarah. He also hired Mysterio to plant the false story and may have even had a Gwen Stacy robot have an affair with his father as part of a demented revenge tale.

Though a convoluted rewrite of the "Sin's Past" storyline, the "Sinister War" retconned the retcon that few ever considered a reasonably sane concept. As shown above, there are means of expanding the Spider-Man origin and legacy that are both enjoyable and reasonable...and there are others that are not

The suggestion of an affair between Gwen Stacy and Norman Osborn resulting in her pregnancy was a rotten idea from the start. It also tainted one of the paramount deaths in Marvel Comics history, that of Gwen Stacy at the hands of the insane Green Goblin. I'm not sure if J. Michael Straczynski's request that Peter Parker be the parent of Sarah and Gabriel Stacy would be any better, but it would certainly be less objectionable from a reader's point-of-view, at least that's what I believe.

As for me, I'm grateful to Nick Spencer for this retcon of a retcon. Normally such twisting of events doesn't sit well with me, but this was different. The "Sin's Past" storyline was poorly conceived and did not add anything of value to the series. This transformation put to rest a shameful chapter of Marvel Comics; one I hope will never be repeated.

Marvel has a habit of periodically rebooting their entire universe for reasons of their own. Occasionally, this happens on a smaller level with an event causing small transformations in a particular character with lesser effects felt by other heroes and villains. In the *Civil War* maxi-series (2006-2007) Peter Parker reveals his identity to the public. To say this shook the Marvel universe is an understatement, but a larger issue emerged a short time later.

Wilson Fisk aka the Kingpin hires a sniper to kill Spider-Man, but Aunt May is the victim. She falls into a coma and is dying, with Stephen Strange, Doctor Doom, Reed Richards, the High Evolutionary, and Doctor Octopus unable to save her life. Assistance arrives in the form of Mephisto, the demon lord who has been tormenting Marvel heroes since *Silver Surfer* #3 (1968). Mephisto appears in the form of a young girl as he begins his manipulation of Spider-Man and the world he exists in at that time.

Mephisto has a very simple deal; he will save the life of May Parker in return for the marriage of Peter Parker and Mary Jane Watson. According to the demonic equivalent of Satan in the Marvel Universe, their love was a great deal more valuable to him than their souls. Mary Jane agrees before Peter can reply and then steps up and whispers something to Mephisto. This will become important later, but for now we fast-forward to the new reality that follows. Peter Parker is living with Aunt May, he and Mary Jane are cold to each other, Harry Osborn is alive after dying in *Spectacular Spider-Man* Vol 1 #200 (1993), new characters such as Lilly Hollister, Carlie Cooper, and Mister Negative are introduced, and nobody remembers Peter Parker is Spider-Man. Oh, and a redheaded heroine named Jackpot has been appearing, making readers suspect she is Mary Jane Watson (she isn't). Mister Negative in particular has since proved an excellent addition to the Marvel Universe. His presence shook up the Mafia tales which had shrunk greatly thanks to writers' overreliance on the Kingpin and the evil Mary-Sue villain, the Hood.

This storyline was soon followed by "Brand New Day," revealing Spider-Man's altered universe. As the story begins, according to reports the hero hasn't been active for one hundred days and a new villain named Menace is terrorizing the city. Soon after, the Spider-Man titles were canceled and only one series ran, *Amazing Spider-Man*, with three issues each month.

Oh, and that secret message Mary Jane whispered to Mephisto? Most thought it was that she would remember everything despite Mephisto's historical rewrite of continuity. In fact, Marvel revealed her statement to the demon king was that she would agree to the deal if Mephisto left Peter Parker alone for the rest of his life. Marvel's Lucifer clone made a very Faustian style response: "Agreed, as far as I'm concerned..." Nice little open doorway for Mephisto, worthy of the devil. As to the child identity he used, that was a projection of what their daughter would look like if they remained together (a classic demonic twist of the knife).

Why did Marvel make such an overwhelming and clunky decision that literally retconned the marriage of Peter and Mary Jane as well as changing the entire Spider-Man universe? Simply put, Marvel editor-in-chief Joe Quesada thought that the idea of a married Spider-Man, whose history is pretty much unbroken since his first appearance, would turn away new readers. He believed being married aged Peter Parker unacceptably and this was the best solution.

Approaching writer J. Michael Straczynski, Quesada proposed his idea, at which time the former added other changes. Straczynski suggested keeping Harry Osborn alive and dating Mary Jane Watson, bringing Gwen Stacy back to life, Spider-Man losing the movie-derived biological webbing he'd been saddled with, and other changes. None of the above was accepted beyond the return of Harry Osborn and the return of the mechanical web shooters. It took a while for the explanation of the alterations to come out, but I won't list them here. Consider it a massive butterfly effect idea, one that took on exponential repercussions over the subsequent history of the hero.

The response to the retcon was fairly uniformly negative, though the art received praise. Overall, the stylistic transformation was clunky and poorly conceived, but quite probably ultimately unimportant. Whether Spider-Man is married or not, writers will probably always drift to bringing Peter Parker and Mary Jane Watson together as a couple. Some of the additions, such as the return of Harry Osborn, the creation of Mister Negative, and other side characters proved acceptable and ultimately fit into the overall continuity of that portion of the Marvel Universe. The Spider-Man newspaper comic strip kept the marriage intact until the conclusion of the series in March 2019. As of this essay's writing, they may or may not be back together, but the marriage idea is probably gone for good.

Personally, I shrugged over this storyline. The wedding of Peter Parker and Mary Jane Watson was a cool idea, but the bizarre obsession it seemed to foster in some writers and artists was kind of creepy in my opinion. Every other issue or so we were "treated" to many nearly nude shots of Mary Jane, making the comics feel like they were written by a scriptwriter from Cinemax After Dark. Also, there were several stalker-style storylines that felt inappropriate at the time and since then, so this era was eliminated. In the end it was an understandable move by Marvel, but one that could have been handled in a better manner. Since that time, the series has moved on and is still a best-selling title.

In modern comics, there are many changes that occur thanks to wholesale transformations of the universes by the choice of management. One of these was the decision to end the Ultimate Universe line, killing most of the heroes in a maxi-series called *Ultimatum*. The universe was still present until the 2015 Marvel event Secret Wars, in which elements of several alternate continuities were merged with that of the 616 universe.

One of the most important concepts that remained was that of the Ultimate universe's second Spider-Man, Miles Morales. Miles received his powers as part of an attempt to recreate Peter Parker's powers. He too was bitten by a genetically transformed spider but didn't want to be a hero. Of African-American and Puerto Rico extraction, his appearance was a surprise that brought many new readers to the comic series.

Miles, having witnessed the Ultimate Spider-Man's death at the hands of the Green Goblin, takes up the mantle of Spider-Man. Originally Peter Parker's family was outraged by the taking of the name and identity, but they quickly grew to accept him and even went so far as to give him Peter Parker's web shooters. Though the Ultimate Peter Parker did return to life, he left the mantle of Spider-Man in the hands of Miles Morales.

At the end of the Secret Wars retcon series in 2015, Molecule Man gives a gift to Miles Morales. He places Miles and his family into the 616 universe, including several who died in the Ultimate Universe. Miles Morales becomes Spider-Man without replacing Peter Parker, allowing them to operate both locally in New York City and in other locations.

Though some were disappointed by the death of the Ultimate Peter Parker, Miles Morales proved a positive addition to the overall Spider-verse. His character was accepted quickly by most readers, who found his different psychological mindset interesting as well as his unique view of the heroes of his world. A major concern of many Marvel fans at the ending of the Ultimate universe was that Miles Morales would be wiped away. Happily, Marvel listened, and the hero exists to this day. He has served as partner to another universe traveling hero, Spider-Woman/Gwen Stacy of Earth-65, the fourth Ms. Marvel Kamala Khan, as well as the Avengers and a new version of the Champions. This open retcon added new elements to the world of Spider-Man and few dislike the idea of a second Spider-Man whose ethnicity is different from the original.

As I stated at the start, the origin of Peter Parker the legendary hero known as Spider-Man remains basically intact. He still received his powers from a radioactive spider, lost his uncle due to his failure to act, and lived with the guilt of his actions from that day forward. What Marvel Comics wisely did over the last sixty years was develop the world around him in directions that were of great impact to the character in a larger sense. The additions may have been good, bad, grotesque, and unpleasant, they do play a larger part in the origin of everyone's favorite wallcrawler.

Frank Schildiner is a martial arts instructor at Amorosi's Mixed Martial Arts in New Jersey. He is the writer of the novels, *The Quest of Frankenstein, The Triumph of Frankenstein, The Spells of Frankenstein, Napoleon's Vampire Hunters, The Devil Plague of Naples, The Land of Everlasting Gloom, The Last days of Atlantis, The Satanic Gangs of New York, Siberian Blood Burn,* and *The Chains of Ares.* Frank is a regular contributor to the fictional series *Tales of the Shadowmen* and has been published in *The Lone Ranger and Tonto: Frontier Justice, The Joy of Joe, Secret Agent X* Volumes 3, 4, 5, 6, and *The Avenger: The Justice Files.* He resides in New Jersey with his wife Gail who is his top supporter and two cats who are indifferent on the subject.

Acknowledgments

First and foremost, a sincere note of appreciation to **Jerry Siegel, Joe Shuster, Bob Kane, Bill Finger, Joe Simon, Jack Kirby, Charles Moulton, Harry G. Peter, Stan Lee**, and **Steve Ditko**. You guys changed my life, and for the better.

In addition, my undying thanks to artist **Jeffrey Hayes** for bringing my cover idea to vibrant life, and to designer **Maggie Ryel,** who somehow always knows exactly what I want these books to look like.

THE "MEMORIES FROM TODAY'S GROWN-UP KIDS" SERIES:

THE JOY OF JOE: MEMORIES OF AMERICA'S MOVABLE FIGHTING MAN FROM TODAY'S GROWN-UP KIDS

"If you grew up as a fan of the 1960s or 1980s versions of GI Joe this is the collection for you... reminiscences that are simultaneously personal and universal no matter your age, location, or childhood experience."
–Amazon Review

RUNNING HOME TO SHADOWS: MEMORIES OF TV'S FIRST SUPERNATURAL SOAP FROM TODAY'S GROWN-UP KIDS

"This book is a great read for fellow Dark Shadows fans. I identified with so many of the thoughts and emotions included in the various essays in this book. Some are funny, some are touching, all are interesting. I highly recommend it!"
–Amazon Review

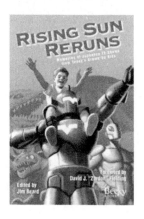

RISING SUN RERUNS: MEMORIES OF JAPANESE TV SHOWS FROM TODAY'S GROWN-UP KIDS

"Outstanding fun read. It'll bring back so many memories of your afternoons after school watching on the old black-and-white television. So well done."
–Amazon Review

Available on
AMAZON.COM

ALSO AVAILABLE FROM

Becky
BOOKS

THE NINE NATIONS BOOK ONE: THE SLIDING WORLD

"This is a quick read, fantasy in the best sense, a remarkable world peopled with mystery, courageous heroes, and dark plots. I tend to read two or three books at a time, but I found myself setting the others aside for this one. Highly recommended!"
–James Stoddard,
Author of the *Evenmere* Series

D.C. JONES AND ADVENTURE COMMAND INTERNATIONAL

"A fun pulp read that felt just like it's meant to feel: Playing with action figures, uncovering mysteries, taking out bad guys with skill and brains. It's a joy and I look forward to the sequels."
–Amazon Review

D.C. JONES AND ADVENTURE COMMAND INTERNATIONAL 2

"The tone of the stories in this volume strikes a perfect balance between action and character, and Beard skillfully gives each member of the Adventure Command distinct and easily identifiable personalities. [The] prose keeps the stories moving at a good clip with snappy dialogue and plenty of action."
–Amazon Review

Available on
AMAZON.COM

Printed in Great Britain
by Amazon

42687066R00099